Echoes from Beyond the Banihal-Kashmir

Human Rights and Armed Forces

Echoes from Beyond the Banihal-Kashmir
Human Rights and Armed Forces

by

Sujata Kanungo

(Established 1870)

United Service Institution of India, New Delhi

Vij Books India Pvt Ltd
New Delhi (India)

Published by

Vij Books India Pvt Ltd
(Publishers, Distributors & Importers)
2/19, Ansari Road, Darya Ganj
New Delhi - 110002
Phones: 91-11-43596460, 91-11- 47340674
Fax: 91-11-47340674
e-mail : vijbooks@rediffmail.com
web: www.vijbooks.com

ISBN: 978-93-81411-42-1

This work is dedicated to the ordinary people of Kashmir who braved many fears to speak for themselves

Contents

List of Maps

List of Tables

Acknowledgement

I extend my sincere gratitude to the United Services Institution of India for granting me the opportunity to carry out this project.

My sincere and profound gratitude goes to His Excellency, Shri N. N. Vohra, Governor, J&K, for the invaluable insights that he had given during our discussion in Srinagar and for the faith he had shown.

Heartfelt gratitude is extended to Shri Omar Abdullah, Chief Minister, J&K, for the time that he spared to have a detailed talk on issues related to the project.

For his benevolence and guidance on the project, I sincerely thank Lt. Gen. Milan Naidu, PVSM, AVSM, YSM (Retd), Member, Armed Forces Tribunal.

Without the help and assistance of the ADGPI's office, Army HQ and the HR Cell (D & V Directorate), Army HQ, this work would remain incomplete. I express my sincere gratitude towards both the Directorates.

Words fall short in expressing my thankfulness to all the officers and men of the Army serving in J&K without whom this project would never take a concrete shape. Thank you all for giving me a peep into your problems and for extending all help and coordination always with a smile.

I express my gratefulness to BSF HQ Kashmir Range and BSF HQ New Delhi, for sharing their views and experiences in the Valley.

Sincere gratitude is expressed towards Mr David Herman (ICRC, Srinagar) and Mr Khurram Parvez (Liaison Officer, IPTK, Srinagar) for the valued insights given by them.

I take this opportunity to express my sincerest gratitude to all those ordinary people of Kashmir without whose cooperation the purpose of this work would be defeated.

This project would not have materialised had it not been for the inspiration and support of Lt. Gen. YM Bammi (Retd). His unrelenting motivation helps me live distant dreams. To him I always owe heartfelt gratitude.

For his calm handling of the hurdles I came across and for the coordination he rendered, I wish to thank Col. S. C. Tyagi (Retd) USI of India.

A special note of thanks goes to my family and friends for always being there for me and being who they are.

It is not possible to name each and every person who has assisted me in his own way towards this project. Last, but not the least, I thank them all.

Introduction

The complexities in the functioning of the twin institutions of Human Rights (HR) and the Armed Forces in low intensity conflicts essentially arise because of the fact that their areas of operation and subject are identical but the mode of achieving results are often in conflict with each other at the ground level.

The Armed Forces are a part of the state machinery and hence have to abide by certain principles which are generally compatible with those of human rights and vice-versa in theory but do not stand good in the thick of counter-insurgency operations. There have been consistent attempts by the Army to accommodate broad measures aimed at sensitising itself to general and basic parameters of human rights, reciprocation thereof for the Armed Forces has been lacking on part of Human Rights Organisations (HROs) . This is apparent from the fact that the latter is known to respond unequivocally with startling immediacy and without caring to verify factual correctness to the alleged plight and suffering of a selected group of people belonging to the civil society and rarely those in the Army.

Extreme political exigencies (insurgency, military, lawlessness etc) which demand on the part of the Armed Forces to adopt measures for countering the same hightens the contradictions between the normal functioning of Armed Forces in such situations and the general codes of the Human Rights apparatus. In conflict zones the operations of the Armed Forces are bound to clash with that of the principles of Human Rights simply because the former is a Central Force and the later a more Universal doctrine. Seemingly the institution of Human Rights cannot for its own functional requirements, include addressing the rights of those employed as Army personnel. The crux of the problem is the question of conflicting functionalities of both the institutions and the resultant lacuna in establishing a general viable administration, security and rights of all groups.

The media often plays a subversive role in its projection of realities as far as cases of violation of Human Rights are concerned. This too is concomitant to the lopsided understanding of Human Rights in a broader perspective where Army personnel are excluded from its purview as being "outside" civil society. This alienates a large section of the Army personnel from the benefits accruing from any functioning HRO and violations of their rights are neither addressed nor projected. One has to remember that their (Army personnel's) fundamental rights to communicate with the press is restricted under the Army Act.

It has been generally seen that the question of Human Rights violations and alleged violations arise in areas where there is maximum insurgency/ terrorism and the Army has been deployed in a low intensity conflict situation. In India glaring examples of such places have been J&K and the North East States of Assam, Nagaland, Manipur and Mizoram.

The very fact of the Army being deployed in a particular state demonstrates that the circumstances prevailing in that state are far from normal. There is a concrete threat to the very lives of the citizenry that the government finds itself unable to deal with. Therefore, acts like the Armed Forces Special Powers Act (AFSPA) (1958) etc were formulated to deal with potentially life threatening situations. In the course of fighting highly motivated and sophistically armed anti-national elements it is desirable to be accepted that the individual rights of the citizens may have to be curtailed to some extent for the preservation of the most basic right – the right to life. Acts like the above mentioned only provide extraordinary powers to deal with an extraordinary situation and the legal immunity required by the Army / SF personnel to operate in situations where a normal recourse in ensuring security to citizens may no longer be an effective option. Curtailment of certain individual rights becomes a functional requirement. It has been noticed that a partial and imperfect understanding of the AFSPA among the general public has led it to be dubbed as 'draconian' and 'anti people'. However, in pursuit of Human Rights the aspect of in-built accountability is often ignored.

Motivation for Research

Born in Shillong, a place known as the Scotland of the East, as a child I and many of my generation have been a witness to violence and curfews in the North Eastern part of the country. I remember distinctly the fear and anxiousness we would experience of being attacked by the majority tribal community in its effort to systematically drive the minority non-tribal community (including mine) out of the tribal land of the Khasi Hills. Our sense of security would each time be reassured when either the CRPF was deployed or on occasions the Army would stage a flag march. Seeing the personnel patrol the streets of our locality, a few of us would run to shake hands with them and exchange pleasantries. Over the years of growing up amid an almost seasonal curfew time, I have seen the confidence and sense of security that the arrival of these men would instill in the otherwise defenseless community. For the protection that they would give to us, the least we could do to express our gratitude was offer the entire picket cups of tea. The ladies never hesitated either to make tea or serve the same to these men. The presence of the security personnel filled us not only with a sense of security but also awe, the awe that the uniform brings with it. Eventually a few from my generation went on to join the Army and serve the nation, not because they did not have any other career option but perhaps to command the same respect and awe. They continue to serve the nation.

Over the years, we have seen more and more insurgent and militant activities in the North Eastern states of Assam, Nagaland, Manipur and the Army and the Para-military forces being deployed. Allegations of Human Rights violation began to be labeled on the security forces who were called in to bring law and order back to the lawlessness of extortion, kidnappings, murders and massacres. They were called in to instill the same confidence and sense of safety and security to thousands of defenseless people. What troubled me from back then till I had undertaken a study, was the image of the Security Forces— disciplined and protectors— that had so deeply embedded itself on the impressionable child's mind. The image that was evolving out of Assam and Jammu and Kashmir in the late 80s and early 90s was that of an insensitive, brutish and rampaging force. Was there a drastic change in the ethos of our Armed Forces ? This conflicting image led me to eventually take up a study of Human Rights and a research, based on the

Armed Forces.

As a student pursuing a Post Graduate Diploma in Human Rights, field trips and research was done from 2007-2008. An unpublished report was submitted to the Indian Institute of Human Rights, New Delhi. As the topic is of extreme importance and relevance, it was deemed necessary to carry out further studies. In my search for finding the truth about various allegations of Human Rights violations labeled on the Indian Army, I had the opportunity of visiting some of the remotest pockets of the country. I had interacted with the local populace during my field trips and got a feel of what reality is and what it is projected to be. My erstwhile field trips were to the south of the Pir Panjal ranges of J&K covering general areas of the Delta Force and Romeo Force under the Northern Command, and 4 Corps under the Eastern Command, with due permission from the then COAS and the facilitation of the Army HQ. During that period, I was unable to visit the most intriguing Kashmir Valley. I had however, carried out some case studies of Human Rights violation and alleged violations pertaining to the Valley. As I felt that a theory and media based study of the complexities of the Valley was inadequate I chose to undertake project to consolidate on previous findings under the aegis of the USI of India.

Significance of the Study

The significance of the study lies in the pertinent questions it raises that have been evaded for long, regarding the very meaning of the term 'Human Rights' as its adherents have deigned it to be. The study also traces the common perceptions about the two titanic institutions of Human Rights Organisation (HRO) and the Army in India where they are brought into conflict on account of their peculiar liberties and rules granted by the same central administration.

The study highlights that while the HRO is a part of a global network of the Human Rights Commission, having certain general principles (operating under the nodal body of the National Human Rights Commission in India) guided by principles of freedom , equality, liberty and right to self determination etc., the Army on the other hand is strictly governed by security concerns which often entail in temporarily restricting certain rights. Hence their interests are often juxtaposed in regionally diverse spaces with insurgent terrorist conditions

The issue of national security and that of basic human rights as has been projected by the media and various NGOs in an often unhealthy and lop-sided 'sensationalist' manner and its ramifications on public perception has also been a concern of the study. There is a need for a more fluid and meaningful interaction and exchange between the Armed Forces and the Human Rights gamut / organisation..

The Study Area

It has been generally observed that the question of human rights violations and alleged violations arise mostly in areas where there is maximum insurgency / terrorism and the Army has been deployed in a low intensity conflict situation. In India glaring examples of such places have been Jammu and Kashmir, the North Eastern states of Assam, Manipur, Nagaland, and Mizoram. (According to a recent report Uttar Pradesh leads the chart of Human Rights violations followed by Gujarat and Delhi).

It would be unjust to say that in states where the a Army is not engaged in such counter insurgency (CI) Ops or counter terrorism (CT) Ops there are no examples of violations of human rights by the state police forces.

However, in the context of violations of human rights by the Army personnel, a study of the trends in the state of J&K covered by the Northern Command of the Indian Army's Operational Command is not only important but intriguing as well.

Jammu and Kashmir for two decades now has been suffering a bloody carnage of militancy/ insurgency with its share of terrorism, exodus of Kashmiri Pundits and other Hindus from the state, loss of lives and property, lack of economic development etc.

The deployment of the Army and Para-military forces to combat armed insurgency and terrorism and such a prolonged exposure to combat has brought it under the ever watchful eyes of various national and international vanguards of Human Rights for violations and alleged violations of Human Rights.

It was thus deemed necessary to see the other side of the coin (here the Army and other SF) to ascertain as to how our troops really function, are expected to function and deal with the additional stress of being labeled 'violators' of the rights of others in dispensing their duty unto death.

Focus of Research

(a) To ascertain on ground the functioning of the Army and SF deployed in Kashmir Valley.

(b) Assess he human aspect of the problem (long drawn operations, lack of public support, intense combat condition and high expectation, separation from families, fear of the unknown, inequality in society etc.

(c) Assess the factors that alienate the Armed Forces the media factor, less interaction, inequality in society etc.

(d) Underline the need for the Armed Forces to be given full rights ie, right to adequate compensation as well as a measure of relaxation in their freedom of speech and expression.

Approach for Research

To establish the above issues, it was felt that a brief introduction to J&K, its people and the rise of militancy was essential.

Thereafter, the rules of engagement of the Army and SF, enabling them to counter militancy was felt, needed to be mentioned and assessed.

The ground reality pertaining to the relation between the Army/ SF and the people of the Valley in the face of militancy and adverse Human Rights violation projection required to be researched as the essence of the work lay in this aspect.

Case studies and the validity of various Human Rights violation allegations had to be undertaken as have been projected by innumerable individuals and HROs.

The roles played by institutions such as the media, state administration, the NHRC and the impact of Operation-Sadbhavna in bringing the situation of the Valley to a near normalcy also merited a study.

Appreciating the role played by the state agencies in bringing things under control and to a position where the state government can take over, a few suggestions have been made for guarding the Human Rights of the people and the Security Forces.

Methodology

The methodology adopted in this work has been that of case study and extensive interactions with the SFs employed in CI Ops in the Valley by visits, interviews and discussions.

Both primary and secondary data have been obtained in the preparation of this project. The primary date sources are :-

(i) Field Trips.

(ii) Discussions.

The secondary data sources are as follows :-

(a) Books.

(b) Journals.

(c) Reports.

(d) Newspapers.

(e) Internet.

Layout of the report

In order to understand the terrain and its people Chapter I contains a brief account of the geography of J&K with particular reference to some of the militancy affected districts of the Valley.

Chapter II gives a brief account of the history of the state from ancient times. It also traces the sufferings, Kashmiris were subjected to at various periods of time.

Chapter III covers the events leading to the rise of insurgency in Kashmir. It also contains a brief account of the various militant groups operating in the Valley.

Chapter IV deals with the circumstances leading to the deployment of the Armed Forces in J&K and their nature of duty in such deployment. An attempt has been made here to understand the various provisions of the Armed Forces Special Powers Act which aids the Armed Forces in CI and CT Ops.

In Chapter V an attempt has been made to explain the restrictions imposed on the troops against causing violations of Human Rights during Ops.

Chapter VI contains a narrative of the views expressed by a cross section of the Kashmiri society with particular reference to the civil society, the state apparatus and the ordinary people of Kashmir on the role played by the Army/ SF over the years. For this purpose public meetings at various locations in the Valley, discussions with the Governor, J&K, Shri NN Vohra, the Chief Minister, J&K, Shri Omar Abdullah, the Liaison Officer, IPTK, Mr Khurram Parvez as also Mr David Herman, ICRC, Srinagar, were undertaken.

Chapter VII attempts to give a first hand account of the problems faced by the troops in combating militants and militancy in population centers. Interaction with the men uniform all across the Valley has helped in the making of the chapter.

Other operations undertaken by the Army in weaning the people away from militancy have been elaborated in Chapter VIII. Goodwill gestures undertaken by the Army under Operation Sadbhavna have been acknowledged here.

Chapter IX covers the judicial roles played by institutions such as the Supreme Court, the Army and the NHRC towards upholding the Rights of the people in the country. This chapter has been included to assure the readers of the provisions of law which hold the Armed Forces accountable of any action which may be termed as a violation of Human Rights.

Chapter X assesses cases of Human Rights violations and alleged violations and the record of the Army in matters of Human Rights with reference to J&K and the North East.

Based on the findings in J&K a number of recommendations and suggestions have been made for future implementation in Chapter XI.

Finally a conclusion has been drawn based on overall findings and assessment of some of the ground realities and the projected versions of the nuances of Human Rights and Armed Forces in J&K.

List of Abbreviations

A

AFSPA	Armed Forces Special Powers Act
APHC	All Party Hurriyat Conference

B

BSF	Border Security Force

C

COAS	Chief of Army Staff
CI	Counter insurgency
CT	Counter terrorism
CM	Chief Minister
CO	Commanding Officer
Cr PC	Criminal Procedure Code

F

FT	Foreign terrorist

H

HRO	Human Rights Organisation

HQ	Headquarters
HM	Hizbul Mujahidin
HUM	Harkat -ul- Mujahidin
HUJI	Harkat –ul- Jihad –e- Islami

I

ISI	Inter Service Intelligence
IPTK	People's Tribunal on Human Rights and Justice in Indian Administered Kashmir
ICRC	International Committee of the Red Cross
ICCPR	International Covenant on Civil and Political Rights

J

J&K	Jammu and Kashmir
JKLF	Jammu Kashmir Liberation Front
JEM	Jaish –e- Mohammad
JEI	Jamaat-e- Islami
JCO	Junior Commissioned Officer
JKCCS	Jammu Kashmir Coalition Society

L

LOC	Line of Control
LeT	Lashkar-e-Toiba

M

MUF	Muslim United Front

N

NHRC	National Human Rights Commission
NGO	Non Governmental Organisation
NCO	Non Commissioned Officer

O

OGW	Over ground worker
Ops	Operations

P

POK	Pakistan Occupied Kashmir

R

RPC	Ranbir Penal Code
RR	Rashtriya Rifles

S

SF	Security Forces
SOP	Standard Operating Procedure
SPO	Special Police Officer

T

TA	Territorial Army

U

UN	United Nations
UDHR	Universal Declaration of Human Rights

W

WO	Warrant Officer

A Brief Introduction to the State of Jammu & Kashmir

Thus wrote the Persian poet Jami, 'Gar Firdaus rôy- e-zamin ast, hamin ast o hamin ast o hamin ast'

The state derives its name from the Sanskrit word Ka (water) and Shamira (to drain) referring thereby to its numerous rivers and streams.

Jammu and Kashmir is internationally bordered by Pakistan, Afghanistan, Russia, China and Tibet. The distinct regions within the state are the Jammu and Kashmir divisions, the Ladakh region and the Northern Areas presently under illegal occupation by Pakistan. The state has an area of 222,236, 2 sq kms. Approximately $1/3^{rd}$ of the area is under the illegal occupation of Pakistan a portion of which she has ceded to China in 1965. Besides, China too is in illegal possession of area in the Aksai Chin region.

As of now J&K has three distinct physical regions comprising the Jammu region South of the Pir Panjal ranges, the Kashmir Valley boundered by the Pir Panjal (in the South) and the Great Himalayan Range to its North and North East and the Ladakh region comprising areas North and North Eastern Himalayas.

The Kashmir Valley is situated at an approximate elevation 1500 m and is about 126 kms in length and 37 kms wide. The main drainage of the Valley is the Jhelum with its tributaries like Lider, Sind, Sandra and Vishwa. It is Jhelum with its tributaries and lakes (Wular, Nagin) that irrigate the fertile alluvial lands of the Valley. The other major rivers that run through the state are Chenab, Ravi, Tawi and Indus originating from the glaciers of the Great Himalayas.

The climate of J&K varies greatly due to the vertical topography. While winters are cold and severe in the Ladakh and Valley regions, summers are hot and humid in the Jammu region especially in Jammu city.

The Kashmir Valley typically enjoys the sub-tropical and temperate type of climate and the natural vegetation consists of cider, oak, walnut, poplars, apple trees etc.

According to the census report of 2001, J&K has a total population of 10,143,700 with maximum density in Kashmir 53.9 per cent, followed by Jammu 43.7 per cent and Ladakh 2.3 per cent .

The Kashmir region has a majority of Muslim population 97.16 per cent , Hindu 1.84 per cent , Sikh 0.88 per cent, Buddhists / others 0.11 per cent.

In Jammu Hindus constitute 65.23 per cent, Muslims 30.69 per cent, Sikhs 3.57 per cent and Buddhist 0.51 per cent . Ladakh has 47.40 per cent , Muslims, 45.87 Buddhists and 6.22 per cent Hindus. According to an estimate by the Central Intelligence Agency about 300,000 Kashmiri Pundits and 50-100000 Kashmiri Muslims from the entire state of J&K have been internally displaced due to the ongoing violence. Claims have been made that J&K is the only Muslim majority state but a closer look at the demographic pattern of Lakshadweep reveals same characteristics.

The principal languages spoken in the state are Kashmiri, Urdu, Dogri, Pahari, Ladaki, Gojri, Balti, Shina and Pashto while Urdu is the official language of the state.

The Kashmir Valley is divided into ten districts viz Baramulla, Kupwara, Bandipora, Anantnag, Pulwama, Budgam, Kulgam, Shopiyan and Srinagar. The author had the opportunity of visiting some of the districts and studying the district profiles and the history of militancy in the same. If the Valley may be divided into three distinct divisions in terms of the area of operation of the Army then in the north we have the Kupwara, Baramulla and Bandipora districts, in the south and central we have the Anantnag, Pulwama, Budgam, Kulgam and Shopiyan districts and the centrally located Srinagar and Ganderbal districts.

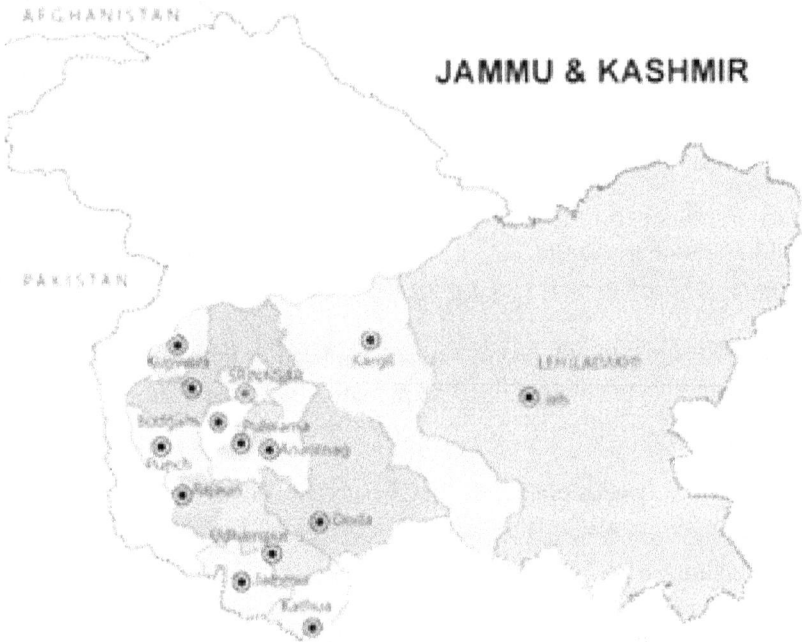

JAMMU & KASHMIR

District Kupwara

Carved out of the Baramulla district in 1979 Kupwara district is situated at an average altitude of 5300 ft above sea level with three Tehsils namely Handwara, Karnah and Kupwara. It consists of 11 blocks: Sogam, Tangdar, Teetwal, Rambal, Kupwara, Rajwal, Kralpora, Langate, Wavoora, Trehgam and Kalaroo and has five assembly constituencies : Karnah, Kupwara, Lolab , Handwara and Langate. Kupwara town is the district HQ and is approx 90 km from Srinagar. Its northern and western borders form the Line of Control (LOC) between India and Pakistan and its eastern and southern borders touch Sopore, Bandipora and Baramulla tehsils (district Baramulla). Through its outer areas flows the Neelum (Kishanganga) river from east to west. The Gabhra pass, Sadham pass and the Nastuchan pass are located in the district. The district abounds in natural beauty especially in the Lolab Valley.

The people are mostly Kashmiri Muslims with a majority of Sunnis with a few Sikhs and Hindus. Gujjar population is found along the border.

District Baramulla

History records Baramulla (city founded by Raja Bhimsina) to be a confluence of all religions. The city had been sacred to Hindus and Buddhists since early times and with the visits of Syed Janbaj Wali (15TH Century) and Guru Hargobind Ji was rendered sacred to all communities.

District Baramulla is the largest in the valley in terms of area (4588 sq kms) and population (11,50,652). It consists of 16 blocks and Tehsils viz Bandipora, Sonawari, Sopore, Baramulla, Gulmarg. The assembly constituencies of the district are Uri, Rafiabad, Sopore, Gurez, Bandipora,Sonawari, Sangrama, Baramulla, Gulmarg and Pattan.

The district shares common boundaries with Kupwara in the North, Poonch and Budgam in the South, the LOC in the West and Srinagar and Ladakh in the East.

Agriculture and livestock rearing form primary occupation of people. Sopore is famous for its apples.

District Anantnag

District Anantnag derives its name from the natural spring of Ananta Naga and is situated in the South Kashmir region. Anantnag houses the famous Amarnath cave and covers an area of 3984 sq kms. Dooru, Kulgam, Bijbera, Pahalgam and Anantnag are the five tehsils of the district. The total population of the district was 11.70 lakhs (2001 census). This district with its Headquarters of Anantnag town attracts thousands of tourists. It is surrounded by the high snow covered peaks of the Himalayan ranges and abounds in natural springs and streams.

Historically this district has been a witness to various changes of rule from Hindu to Mughal and thereafter. The temples, shrines and springs are popular among the followers of the Hindu religion.

District Budgam

Budgam was carved out from the Srinagar district in 1979. It is surrounded by the districts Baramulla, Srinagar and Pulwama. District Budgam comprises of six Tehsils viz Budgam, Beerwah, Chadoora, Chari-e-sharief,Khag and Khan Sahib and consists of 496 villages. Its population as per 2001 census is 29 lakhs. It is located at an average height of 5281 ft above sea level and covers an area of 1371 sq kms. The climate is mainly temperate. The northern parts of the district are mainly plain while the southern and south western parts are hilly. The district abounds in tourist destinations of both natural beauty and historical significance.

District Pulwama

Spread over 698 kms, Pulwama district was carved out of the Anantnag district in 1979. It is subdivided into four tehsils, six community development blocks. 554 villages house a total population of 6.49 lakhs (Census 2001). Cultivation of rice is the primary occupation of the people. The land also yields pulses, paddy, maize, mustard etc. Besides, this district is famous for its saffron cultivation around Pampore and the ambree apples. Approximately 1011 sq kms of the district is forested.

Shopiyan

Shopiyan was accorded a district status in 2007. It is located 54 kms from Srinagar and is at an average height of 6748 ft above sea level. Named after Sheen-e-Van meaning forest of snow, it has historical importance attached to it due to the Mughal Road. Shopiyan has two Assembly constituencies viz Wachi and Shopiyan. The district abounds with apple orchards. There is cultivation of paddy, maize and jawar. Besides cultivation, other sources of income are the service sector and cottage industry sector. The district has potential for the development of tourism.

A Brief Outline of the History of Jammu & Kashmir

Having taken an account of the geographical aspect it becomes important to take a peek into the reasons for the mushrooming of secessionist and violent tendencies in the ancient and peaceful land of Kashmir.

Since time immemorial Kashmir was a centre of Indo-Vedic culture and civilisation. There is recorded history of Kashmir in the Purans which traces the origin of Kashmir and its earliest ruler. History of Kashmir is also recorded during the Mahabharata period and the Mauryan period.

Kashmir during the rule of Kanishka was the seat of Mahayana Buddhism.In Kanspura town many Buddhist Viharas were built by Kanishka. Lalitaditya was the most renowned king of Kashmir who ruled over it in the seventh century. The last Hindu ruler of Kashmir was Sahdev who ascended the throne in 1301 AD.

During the reign of Sahdev, Rinchan a Buddhist Bhotia entered into his service and eventually usurped the throne of Kashmir for himself. Being denied conversion to Shaivism, Rinchan converted to Islam and ruled for three years until 1323 AD.

Udyan Dev, the brother of Sahdev ascended the throne after the death of Rinchan but could not rule for long. Shahmiri, a Muslim adventurer who had also entered into the service of Sahdev soon overthrew Udyan Dev. Thus began the 200 year of Muslim rule over Kashmir in 1339 AD.

The fourth ruler of the Shahmiri dynasty Sikander who came to be known as 'But-Shikan' (destroyer of idols) followed a fanatical policy of conversion of his subjects into Islam. Most of the Hindus were converted or put to death. Very few could escape this reign of terror. He destroyed almost all Hindu temples. Along with his Chief Minister Saif-ud-Din (himself a convert) Sikander is believed to have burnt seven mounds of sacred threads of murdered Brahmins and thrown into the Dal Lake along with sacred books of the Hindus.[1]

Sikander's successor Zain-ul-Abidin brought in a change. He not only stopped forced conversions but also recalled the Hindus who had fled to their homeland. For his effective administration and developmental work Zain-ul-Abidin earned the reputation of the greatest Sultan of Kashmir.

The Shahmiri dynasty was replaced by the Chak dynasty in 1561 and eventually in 1589 AD Kashmir came under the Mughal rule as a province of the Mughal empire.

The Mughal reign under Akbar and Jehangir was generally peaceful but atrocities were committed on the Hindus during the reign of Aurangzeb. One of his Governors persecuted the Brahmins who turned towards Guru Tegh Bahadur for help. The Guru's statement to them infuriated imperial Court and led to his martyrdom.

After the death of Aurangzeb the Mughals lost the central control over Kashmir which then came under the Afghans. With the advent of the Afghans under Ahmad Shah Abdali, Kashmir was all set to witness the most cruel and brutal of times. More than 60 years of Afghan rule caused the Kashmiri people untold miseries. Afghan Chiefs Abdullah Khan Isk Aquasi, Lal Khan Khattak, Faqirullah were famous for their notoriety and brutal means of subjugation of the Kashmiri people. Amir Khan Jawnsher a fanatic Shia Afghan governor had declared himself independent and upon doing so persecuted the Sunnis. During the Governorship of Haji Karim Dad Khan, Asad Khan, Ata Muhammad Khan, the people of Kashmir suffered immensely. These Afghans would do anything to oppress the Kashmiris - loot, plunder, kill, sexually abuse – just about anything.

---

[1] Kashmir – The Storm Center of The World – Bal Raj Madhok

The last of the Afghan tyrant was Jabbar Khan who persecuted the Hindus. So brutal were the Afghans in their ways that Birbal Dhar, a Pundit nobleman approached Maharaja Ranjit Singh for help.

The Sikhs who had earlier attempted to capture Kashmir were in 1819 able to do so under the command of Misser Dewan Chand. Kashmir then became a province of the Lahore Kingdom.

In 1846 Kashmir passed on to the hands of Raja Gulab Singh a powerful Dogra functionary in the Lahore Kingdom. With the help of his officer Zorawar Singh, Gulab Singh had captured Ladakh and Baltistan regions as well. In the aftermath of the Anglo-Sikh war the heavy financial demands of the British and the straitened circumstances of the Sikh rulers allowed Gulab Singh to establish himself as the Kashmiri sovereign by making a payoff to the British. Thus established, the Dogra dynasty lasted for a little over a century. This period saw four rulers – Gulab Singh (1846-57), Ranbir Singh who added the emirates of Humza, Gilgit and Nagar to the Kingdom (1857-85), Pratap Singh (1885-1925) and Hari Singh (1925-52). During the Rising of 1857 the princely state of Kashmir sided with the British and with the subsequent assumption of direct rule by Great Britain came under the paramount of the British crown. The state acceded to India on October 26, 1947 and the hereditary rule of the Dogras was abolished in 1952. Till 1947 the British held a sway over all the Dogra rulers.

The circumstances that led to the end of the Dogra rule and gave rise to the Kashmir problem can be traced to the new political and social awakening in J & K. On the other hand the Indian freedom movement was gaining momentum under the Indian National Congress with the emergence of the Muslim League too.

The Great Indecision of 1947

At the time of the conclusion of British rule and partition of Indian Empire into India and Pakistan. Hari Singh was the reigning king of J&K. Both Pakistan and India had agreed that the princely states would be given the option to join either side based on communal contiguity or in special cases to remain independent. Kashmir at the time had a Muslim majority population ruled by a Hindu King. Jinnah claimed Kashmir for Pakistan on the ground of it being a Muslim state. To postpone making a hurried decision, while tossing with the idea to remain independent Hari Singh signed a 'stand still' agreement with Pakistan. Any such agreement was pending with India. In October 1947 tribals from the North West Frontier Province (NWFP) led by regulars supported by Pakistan government invaded Kashmir. The aim of the campaign was to capture Kashmir Valley and the capital city Srinagar as also frighten Hari Singh to submission. Instead, Hari Singh appealed to Lord Mountbatten, the Viceroy of India, for assistance. Lord Mountbatten agreed to help on the condition that the ruler accede to India. Once the Instrument of Accession was signed by Hari Singh, Indian soldiers landed in Kashmir and successfully drove out the intruders from all but a small section of the state. Pakistan has since been treating the accession as a fraudulent transaction.

In the fighting that followed the UN was requested to intervene. The then Prime Minister of India Pandit Nehru, himself a Kashmiri, approached the UN for a resolution of the problem and mooted the question of ascertaining the wishes of the people about the accession to India. This complicated the issue which otherwise was legally and constitutionally settled by the acceptance of the Instrument of Accession by the head of the princely state. However, India insisted that no referendum could be held till all of the state was cleared by the intruders and law and order established.

Post 1947

In 1948, a ceasefire was agreed upon under the aegis of the UN. At the time of ceasefire Pakistan had gained illegal possession of Gilgit, Baltistan including the Muzaffarabad region and till date maintains so. The area under its occupation has come to be called POK. The UN passed four resolutions with regard to the J&K issue. The third resolution is very significant in that it related to the ceasefire, made it mandatory for Pakistan to withdraw all its forces regular and irregular from occupied territory and India to reduce the strength of its forces present in J&K. Lastly, the future status of J&K was to be determined by a plebiscite supervised by the UN. Pakistan has not withdrawn her troops from the areas illegally occupied by her as per the resolution. Thus, India has opposed a referendum which could be held only after Pakistan has fully vacated Kashmir.

In 1949, the government of India (through the machinations of Pandit Nehru) yielded the reigns of the state government to Sheikh Abdullah, the leader of National Conference (erstwhile Muslim Conference) after the ouster of Maharaja Hari Singh. Having been defeated in the 1947-48 war and having failed to capture the Valley, since 1948 Pakistan has made two major attempts to wrest the region by launching military operations in 1965 and 1971 but failed. Between 1980 – 1990 the internal situation in the Valley deteriorated due to political and bureaucratic problems. Taking advantage of the turmoil in the Valley, Islamabad lured innocent and unemployed Kashmiri youth across the LOC in POK, established camps and trained them as militants, armed and misguided them to launch a revolt against the Centre.

The deep seated conflict / dispute over Kashmir led to the rise of militancy in the state that saw a peculiar intensification in 1989.

The Sheikh Abdullah Factor

Sheikh Muhammad Abdullah, christened the Sher-e-Kashmir (Lion of Kashmir) was a scion of Kashmiri Brahmin family converted to Islam in the 18th Century. He was the most dominant leader that Kashmir has ever had in the pre and post Independence era.

The subjugated Kashmiri people over centuries of oppressive rule acquired the crafty image of a lazy and uneducated lot especially the non-artisan class. It was Sheikh Abdullah who played the lead role in the political and social re-awakening of the people. He was almost the face of Kashmir from 1939 until his death in 1982. Born in 1905, he passed his B.Sc from Islamia College, Lahore and his M Sc (Chemistry) from Aligarh Muslim University in 1930. In 1931 he was made the leader of the Jammu and Kashmir Muslim Conference to lead the agitation against the Maharaja. He was projected as the leader of the Muslim majority in Kashmir and soon gained mass support. In 1939 Sheikh Abdullah opened the doors of Muslim conference to non-Muslims converting it to National Conference – a more secular front on the lines of the Indian National Congress. Kashmir's politics took a new turn in 1942 when the National Conference began tilting towards communism. The communist elements wanted to make independent Kashmir a launch pad for the spread of communism in the rest of the country.

Sheikh Abdullah flaunted dreams of an independent Kashmir of which he would be the undisputed leader. In 1946 Sheikh Abdullah made a public call to the Maharaja to quit Kashmir and propagated his people to do everything to end the Dogra rule. He was arrested and violence arson gripped the Valley thereafter. Abdullah was tried and sentenced to imprisonment and was thus for three years absent from the picture till August 1947. The objective of Abdullah as many believe was to establish an independent Kashmir under his tutelage or Sheikhdom. Abdullah they believe seemed concerned only about the Valley and its Muslims neglecting the interests and welfare of the people of Jammu and Ladakh. Though Sheikh Abdullah enjoyed a close rapport with Jawahar Lal Nehru, his relation with Jinnah had soured following his refusal to merge the National Conference with the Muslim Conference of Chowdhary Ghulam Abbas. Nehru's relation with Abdullah and his personal moorings over Kashmir allowed the latter to almost always have his way and the root of most of Kashmir's problems ever-since. Following the arrest of the Sheikh in 1946, Nehru himself proceeded to Kashmir to make arrangements for the former's defence much against the prohibitory orders the Maharaja. He was arrested at Pattan Bridge – an event that soured Nehru's relation with the Maharaja. The bitterness between Abdullah and Jinnah, between Abdullah and the Maharaja, between Nehru and the Maharaja had adverse effect on the polity of the state of J&K.

Sheikh Abdullah who headed the Emergency Administration consequent to the accession of J&K to India was appointed the Prime Minister with a Council of Ministers in 1948 much with the support of Nehru. In 1949 upon a proclamation vesting powers on his son Karan Singh, the Maharaja abdicated the throne and the state. Sheikh Abdullah took all decisions of the state even though there was an elected legislature and sidelined Karan Singh.

By 1952 Sheikh Abdullah's aspiration to have an independent Kashmir beneath his pro-India stance began to discomfort the Central leadership. In his speeches he denunciated the Indian government, press and even declared that the interference of the Central government in the affairs of Kashmir would not be tolerated. He exploited the inability of India to hold the plebiscite and "differences arose between him and the Central leaders particularly in regard to the issues of fundamental rights, citizenship, jurisdictional of the Supreme Court, Election Commission, emergency powers etc". As a step to resolve such unwarranted differences a broad agreement known as the Delhi Agreement was arrived at in July 1952 which was soon approved by the Constituent Assembly of the State.

Besides various other provisions, the Agreement allowed the flying of a separate flag for the state beside the national flag subject to certain restrictions and limitations. The Constituent Assembly went on to abolish the hereditary monarchy thereafter and vide a formal resolution the head of the state was designated as the Sadar-i-Riyasat who was to be elected by the State Legislative Assembly for a period of five years.

The Delhi Agreement came under severe criticism from the Praja Parishad in Jammu which felt that the Sheikh was unduly being appeased by Nehru. At the national level the Jana Sangh supported the agitation. Analysts feel that provisions of the Agreement which suited him such as the abolition of the hereditary monarchy were implemented immediately while other items were reserved to be implemented later.

Till his dismissal and arrest in 1953, Sheikh Abdullah being encouraged by the Anglo-US bloc spoke vehemently for an independent Kashmir causing concerns to the Central leadership. Sheikh Abdullah was released in 1958 and re-arrested the same year charged with conspiracy under the Kashmir conspiracy case. Sheikh Abdullah's Prime Minister-ship was replaced by his deputy Prime Minister Bakshi Ghulam Mohammad who was an effective leader. He resigned in 1963, the same year as the theft of the hair of Prophet Mohammed – the Holy Relic. In the intermittent period Kashmir saw two Prime Ministers in Shamsuddin and Ghulam Mohammad Sadiq. During the tenure of Sadiq the titles of Prime Minister and Sadar-i-Riyasat were changed to Chief Minister and Governor respectively. Sadiq who took over office in 1964 remained the Chief Minister till 1971. In 1964, following the withdrawal of the conspiracy case against him by Nehru and Sadiq, Sheikh Abdullah made trips to foreign countries including China and indulged in political propaganda and upon his return was arrested.

The Indo-Pak war of 1965 cooled the heels Sheikh Abdullah and the political atmosphere in the Valley. Pakistan learnt that any attempt to grab

Kashmir would cost her heavy. In 1967 Abdullah was released and in 1971 along with the Mirza Afzal Beg and GM Sadiq was expelled from the state. The plebiscite Front (founded by Mirza Afzal Beg in 1955 with the blessings of Sheikh Abdullah) which continued its activities with vigour was also banned in 1971.

During the Bangladesh war of 1971 Pakistan again tried to grab Kashmir but after its forces surrendered in Bangladesh, accepted to ceasefire on December 17. Subsequent to the war the Shimla Agreement was signed between India and Pakistan in 1972 in which the two countries resolved to settle their differences bilaterally through peaceful means.

Witnessing the defeat of Pakistan and the signing of the Shimla Agreement, the attitude of leaders like Sheikh Abdullah and Mirza Afzal Beg underwent a change. The flavour of the change was conciliatory and the zeal to have an independent Kashmir retarded. This was the time when the then Prime Minister Mrs Indira Gandhi arrived at a settlement with Sheikh Abdullah, thus the Kashmir Accord was signed. Keeping the spirit of the Accord, Sheikh Abdullah was elected the leader of the Congress Legislative Party and sworn in as the Chief Minister in 1975. Earlier Chief Minister Syed Mir Qasim who had taken over as Chief Minister after the death of Sadiq in 1971 was made to resign.

The relation between the Congress and Sheikh Abdullah was that of love and hate and did not last long. Sheikh Abdullah revived the National Conference and functioned as its president while holding office on the support of another political party. 1975 was also the year when Sheikh Abdullah dissolved the Plebiscite Front and merged it with the National Conference. The Parliamentary elections of 1977 ousted the Congress at the Centre and the Congress withdrew its support to the Legislative Assembly in Kashmir. Sheikh Abdullah sought the dissolution of the Assembly. The Janata Party wave that had swept over the Parliamentary elections failed to capture J&K and more specifically the Valley in the Legislative Assembly elections owing to the lack of a clear mandate in the state. The Congress party suffered a great defeat and eventually Sheikh Abdullah and his National Conference came to power. The spectacular victory almost made Sheikh Abdullah an authoritarian delegating powers and offices to a hand-picked few thus corrupting and corroding influences. The Sheikh ignited the Resettlement Bill issue and kept the masses on his side and support. He also paved the way for his son Dr Farooq Abdullah to take on the reigns after him.

Thus leading an eventful life, Sheikh Abdullah passed away in 1982. Dr Farooq Abdullah succeeded him as the Chief Minister with behind the scene support of Mrs Indira Gandhi. The elections of 1983 saw conflicts between the Congress and the National Conference and the relation between the Centre and the State became tense. Anti-national activities started gaining momentum and violent disturbances increased.

3 Genesis of the Kashmir Insurgency

The ramifications of the historical indecisions, blunders, personal ambitions and illusions over and in Jammu and Kashmir found a new direction and fervor in the mid 1980s when militancy set a foot hold in the Kashmir Valley. Propelled by the sinister design of Pakistan and nurtured by the pro Pakistan elements within the Valley this virus had began to infest itself in every organ of the state machinery – leading to its eventual collapse.

The employment of fascist techniques, exploitation of religions and regional feelings for political gains led to the rigged election of 1983. The fire was fanned conveniently by anti-Centre, pro-plebiscite and communal sentiments by the joining of hands of the National Conference and Mirwaiz Moulvi Farooq. Going by the version of none other than Mr Jagmohan "Dr Farooq Abdullah spoke different languages at different places".[1]

The result of all this was a clear divide within J&K on communal and parochial lines.

The security environment during that period was marked by a series of bomb blasts and presence of anti-national elements. The ugly incidences of subversion during Independence day celebrations, one-day international cricket match between India and West Indies (Oct 13, 1983), the kidnapping and murder of Ravindra Mhatre (February 1984) by J&K Liberation Army (the militant organ of the Plebiscite Front) and the fall out of the execution of Maqbool Butt on February 11, 1984 were indicators of what lay in store for the future if no action was taken and invariably the tension that prevailed

---

[1] My Frozen Turbulence in Kashmir – Chapter VII, Tension Ridden Atmosphere Pg 269.

in the state. The news of Muslim and Sikh youths indulging in subversive activities was another cause of security concern. Violent processions targeted security personnel, vehicles and shops, houses and temples were attacked and gutted. A number of other subversive activities by anti-national elements dotted the period 1983-84.

On the political front bickerings and ambitions within the National Conference and Congress (I) circle could have given no more to the state and its people but instability, mismanagement and mal-administation. Both Dr Farooq Abdullah and GM Shah wanted the seat of Chief Minister secured for themselves. The latter even opposed to the former's claims to party leadership. The Congress (I) on the other hand initiated public agitation against the misrule of Dr Farooq Abdullah. The Central Government worried over the liaison that had developed between the subversive elements in the Punjab and J&K [2]. There were concerns regarding the secessionists and Pro-Pak elements in the Valley but the political leaders in the state seemed far from paying heed to the danger signs.

The atmosphere in the Valley was charged and tensed – political and administrative tensions, tensions caused by anti-national rather pro-Pak and pro-Khalistan elements.

The defection of GM Shah with the support of 12 members of the Legislative Assembly in July 1984 led to the dismissal of Farooq Abdullah as the Chief Minister. The then Governor, Mr Jagmohan had outlined the necessity of the imposition of Governor's Rule during the intervening period citing the threat to law and order and security of the state by 'disruptionists' as also the political instability. The Union government turned down the request leading to the swearing in GM Shah as the new Chief Minister with the support of 12 members of the Legislative Assembly and the external support of 26 Congress legislators.

The communal violence of 1986 in Kashmir in which thousands of Hindus were rendered homeless bolstered the communal policies which GM Shah is known to have played in the state.

---

[2] My Frozen Turbulence in Kashmir, Pg 299

The GM Shah Government was dismissed in 1986 and Governor's Rule was imposed. During Governor's rule the political task of defeating the conspiracy of destabilising the society through acts of violence and subversion adopted by the fundamentalists and communalists was somewhat achieved.

With the rounding up of pro-Khalistani and pro-Pak elements as well as anti-social elements the 'sources of mischief were immobilised'. Contrary to popular belief or the belief of convenience, the period of Governor's Rule witnessed development and good administration.

The election of 1987 in J&K saw the forging of alliance between Dr Farooq Abdullah's National Conference and Congress (I) led by Rajiv Gandhi on the one hand while on the other pro-Pak Islamic groups and parties under the banner of Muslim United Front (MUF) joined hands. The MUF was dominated by Jamaat-e-Islami. In its election manifesto the MUF pledged to free the Muslims of Kashmir from the Hindu rule of India and 'campaigned on anti-India fundamentalist platform'.[3]

Though the MUF mastered only four seats and alleged that the election was rigged, it had none-the-less set a trend of openly voicing anti-India sentiments in the garb of freedom of political expression.

Dr Farooq Abdullah again assumed the office of the Chief Minister forming a coalition government but faced stiff opposition of MUF and 'hostility of Kashmiri Muslims'. Once again he spoke in different languages in different places – while in the Valley he turned to Islamic fundamentalists, in Jammu he posed as a secularist. Once again he tried to win the support of the Khalistani elements.

Now, with an elected government in place, the year 1988 witnessed wide spread violence all across the state of Jammu and Kashmir . There was large scale violence and public disorder leading to the loss of innocent lives and property. Exfiltration of Kashmiri youth across the border to receive arms training and infiltration of armed militants owing allegiance to various subversive groups gained pace. The undercurrent subversion coupled with

---

[3] Kashmir : Storm Centre of the World, Pg 1704.

fanaticism and fundamentalism had began to take in its stride the social, political and administrative set-up of the state in general and the Valley in particular. Bomb blasts, dacoity, arson, processions, riots, violent clashes causing deaths and countless injuries to civilians were the hallmarks of the year. The death of General Zia-ul-Haq in Pakistan became yet another reason for rioting in Srinagar and elsewhere in the Valley. There were clashes between Shias and Sunnis following which the Moharram procession had to be abandoned.

Frenzied crowds would often take to the streets breaking curfew rules again leading to clashes between them and Police which resorted to firing to disperse the crowd.

Was the issue Azaadi or was it the desire of the entire people of the Valley to merge with Pakistan ? Were the actions of the people manifestations of exploitative and medieval policies? Not long before 1988 the same people had voted in favour of one political party or the other. In hind sight the answer seems to be hidden in the last question. One cannot agree more with Mr Jagmohan when he says "All the local groups and regional parties rely, not on hard and honest work to win over the Kashmiri masses, but on emotive and medieval issues to prop up their political standing. In this attitude lies the fundamental malady of Kashmir's polity and administration. Instead of grappling with the reality and tackling the problem from its roots, short-cuts are resorted to and personality-oriented politics is encouraged".[4]

The year 1988 witnessed another significant development in the security parlance , that of the launch of a well planned strategy by General Zia-ul-Haq after the withdrawal of Russian forces from Afghanistan . The strategy as it unfolded allowed a three phase plan of execution. In its first phase the agenda was the spread of a low key insurgency to keep the administration of J&K under siege and to subvert the police forces, financial institutions and other key apparatus. This phase had as its aim to whip up anti India feelings in the youth and the peasants, exploiting religious issues and to create terror and chaos to begin with.

---

[4] My Frozen Turbulence in Kashmir , Pg 114.

The second phase of the plan was to "exert maximum pressure on Siachen-Kargil and Rajouri-Poonch sectors"[5] to divert the attention of the Indian Army from the Kashmir Valley. Ambitious plans were drawn up to destroy bases, depot and headquarters at Srinagar, Pattan, Kupwara, Baramulla, Bandipora and Chowkibal by covert action and finally attack and destroy airfields, radio stations and vital links to the Kashmir Valley.

The third phase aimed to liberate Kashmir and establish an independent Islamic state.

General Zia had spelt out the need for the quick implementation of the plan before the general elections in India and before the military reserves engaged in Sri Lanka could become available.

The large scale subversive and violent activities which continued unabated throughout 1988-89 was well according to the designs of phase one of the plan. The various apparatus of the state machinery was infested by the worms of subversion and terrorism leading to its decay and eventual collapse. The events of the year as recorded by the then Governor of J&K, Mr Jagmohan in 'My Frozen Turbulence in Kashmir' authenticate the anarchy, terror and inactions that prevailed and the danger that was looming large over the Valley, believed to be the abode of Rishi Kashyap.

Since on the political front lack of developmental activities, corruption, mal-administration and unemployment had led to disillusionment and frustration amongst the youth, the timing of the launch of the ambitious plan General Zia could not have been better. Pakistan was out to avenge the defeat suffered by her in the war of 1971 and this time round plans were to "Bleed India with thousand cuts". Religious fundamentalism was infused as one of the weapons in this cost effective and undeclared Proxy War against India in Kashmir in the name of Jihad which had gained Pakistan wide support from Islamic countries in the War in Afghanistan.

Batches of disgruntled Kashmiri youth were indoctrinated, given training in and arms and explosives handling under the patronage of the Pak army and ISI in POK and sent back to wage a "Holy War" or Jihad.

—————————————————————————

[5] Kashmir : Storm Centre of the World, Pg 1708.

They were also to receive support of foreign mercenaries such as from Afghanistan, Sudan, Libya, Iraq, Iran and Pakistan of course. Initially these youths got wide support from the masses and were hailed as liberators and heroes. As has been said by someone "insurgency is a fish that swims in the waters of mass support", the movement in Kashmir set a smooth sail in the late 80s.

The political machinery came to a virtual collapse leading to the proclamation of Governor's Rule in 1990 and the deployment of large number of troops both Army and Para-Military (BSF in particular), to counter a situation where on one hand the state Police force was as good as defunct and a 'War' being waged on the other hand .

Mr Jagmohan who had taken over as the Governor for the second time called upon the Army to restore law and order in the restive border state of J&K where insurgency had turned into militancy. Carrying out the War were multiple militant organisations in various districts of the Valley. It becomes pertinent here to have a bird's eye view of what the Army was and still is in for. The ideologies of the various militant groups operating then and even now- their guiding factors, motivation and aspirations – that determine their tactics, weaponry and manoeuvre are briefly spelt below.

Peep Into The Ideologies Of Various Tanzeems (Militant organizations)

From the time insurgency took a turn towards militancy some of the following groups have been operating in the Valley and have also spread their influence beyond the Pir Panjal ranges. While some have followed the doctrine of Islamisation using terror to ultimately merge J&K with Pakistan, others have been interested in liberating Kashmir from Indian rule through an armed struggle. In this light, one can broadly categorise the Tanzeems into two genres viz the Pro-Pakistan and the Pro-independence groups.

It is believed that LeT has split into two groups Al Mansurin and Al Nasirin. The save Kashmir Movement, Harkat-ul-Mujahidin, Freedom Force, Farzandan-e-Milat, Al Badr, Jaish-e-Mohammad, Hizbul-Mujahidin are currently active in the Valley. The All Party Hurriyat Conference (APHC) that apparently uses moderate means to press for the rights of the Kashmiri people is often considered as a mediator between militant groups and New Delhi. It is believed that the United Jihad Council (formed under the directions of the ISI) acts as an umbrella for all militant groups operating in the Valley and aids collaboration between various groups. Some of the dominant groups operating are Al Badr, Lashkar-e-Toiba (LeT), Jaish-e-Mohammad (JEM), Harkat-ul-Mujahidin (HUM), Hizbul-Mujahidin (HM), Jamait-ul-Mujahideen, Muslim Janbaaz Force, and Dukhtaran-e- Millat etc. There are at least 35 to 36 groups active in Kashmir.

Jammu Kashmir Liberation Front

Though reduced in importance the Jammu Kashmir Liberation Front (JKLF), with Yaseen Malik as its prominent leader, advocates absolute independence for J&K.

Jaish-e-Mohammad (JEM)

The JEM comprising mostly of Pakistanis owing allegiance to Sunni sectarian outfit, advocates the liberation of J&K through armed struggle.

Ikhwaan-ul-Musalmeen

A splinter group of the JKLF, Ikhwaan-ul-Musalmeen is known to have worked in harmony with the HM and JKLF with a pro-Pakistan stance.

Lashkar-e-Toiba (LeT)

The most fanatic and fundamentalist group known for its notoriety, the LeT aims to wage Jihad and merge J&K with Pakistan. It constitutes mostly of foreign terrorists (FTs) and is believed to be directly under the operational control of the ISI. It jointly operates with HM and JEM in Kashmir.

Hizbul Mujahidin (HM)

The armed wing of the Jammait-e-Islami, HM consists of well motivated and indoctrinated cadres and is believed to be the strongest operating group though in recent years it has suffered major blows with the neutralisation of most of its top rank cadres. This group aims for a merger of J&K with Pakistan.

Al Badr

Al Badr's political agenda and ideology lies in that it wants the merger of J&K with Pakistan.

Harkat-ul-Mujihidin (HUM)

Comprising mostly of FTs, the HUM aims to establish supremacy of Islam all over the world.

Harkat-ul-Jihad-e-Islami (HUJI)

HUJI consisting primarily of FTs is an Islamic fanatic group having for its political front the Jamait-ulema-islami.

Jamait-ul-Mujahidin and Others

A Pro-Pakistan group the Jamait-ul-Mujahideen consists mostly of FTs. On similar lines are the Jehrik-ul-Mujahideen (having tie ups with LeT) comprising also mostly of FTs are Al Jehad, Tehriq-e-Jehad etc.

Al Barq

Al Barq supports the UN resolution on J&K and acceptance of J&K as a disputed territory.

Dukhtaran-e-Millat

Dukhtaran-e-Millat or Daughters of Islam aims to establish an Islamic state in J&K. This one of its kind group is known for imposing crude medieval Islamic diktats on women in especially the Valley region and also working as OGWs or conduits. This organisation has been by and large successful in getting the women folk to participate not only in agitational protests and the chest beating "Hai Hais" but also in delay, hindrance and complications in various security operations.

Jamaat-e-Islami (JEI)

Radical Islamisation and use of violent Jihad have been the hallmarks of the Jamait-e-Islami which has been the primary "instrument for executing Pakistan sponsored Proxy War".[6]

---

[6] War against insurgency and terrorism in Kashmir – Lt Gen YM Bammi.

All Party Hurriyat Conference (APHC)

A conglomeration of various local parties (political and militant) the APHC is believed to be backed by Pakistan. All terrorist groups and organizations combine and give a united political front under the aegis at the APHC which has SAS Geelani as its prominent hardline leader. Following differences of opinion and ideals the APHC has split with the moderate faction being led by Mirwaiz Umar Farooq. The Hurriyat has often shied away from (desists) any political dialogue with New Delhi (the most recent example can be seen as in the aftermath of the flare up in the Valley in 2010) and claims to be the sole representative of the people of J&K.

As directed by its Pakistani mentors the Hurriyat "insists on resolution of the Kashmir problem in conjunction with the people of POK and wants Pakistan's participation in any solution". [7] Under the direction of ISI all terrorist organizations take orders from hardliner Geelani who is also believed to be in full control of funds. The summer flare up of 2010 also witnessed the rise of a probable hardline successor of Geelani.

Established with the aim to give a political thrust to insurgency, the AHPC has been most vocal against security forces and in raising Human Rights issues to International Human Rights bodies.

Over the years since 1994 the Hurriyat has displayed a lack of cohesiveness. Major dissensions have been caused by "pro-Islamic" Pak hawk Geelani and pro-independence moderates like Yaseen Malik.

Command and control of FTs especially Pakistan based ones, the allegations of siphoning of funds and arms and ammunition are some of the other factors responsible for a lot of squabbling within the Hurriyat. However, all factions of the Hurriyat get funds from Pakistan and most of its leaders live in palatial bungalows.

Areas of Operation of some of the major Tanzeems

The JKLF exercised much influence and drew a most of its cadre from Kupwara. Through the years elements of HM, HUM, LeT, JEM and others

[7] War against insurgency and terrorism in Kashmir – Lt Gen YM Bammi.

have been operating in North Kashmir. Though most of the Tanzeems comprise of majority of local terrorists others especially the LeT comprises mostly of FTs.

KUPWARA

SOPORE

BARAMULA

PULWAMA

SHOPIAN

REASI

JAMMU

SRINAGAR

BUDRAM

TRAI

ANANTNAR

KISHTWAR

DODA

BHADERWAH

NOT TO SCALE

Outline Sketch of Jammu And Kashmir

Being a border district Baramulla has been one of the major infiltration and exfiltration routes. Areas like Sopore, Baramulla, Handwara are Islamic dominated by the JEI and MUF and are particularly known for being the hard-liner Pro-Pakistani hotbeds. The HM, LeT, JEM, HUJI etc are some of the dominant militant groups in the Baramulla district.

Elements of HM, LeT and JEM are active in Anantnag, Budgam and Shopiyan while the HUM makes its presence felt in Pulwama besides the former mentioned groups. (Refer to Annexure 1 for details on fatalities caused by militants).

4 Deployment of the Army, Para Military Forces and Their Nature of Duty

Until its deployment in 1990 in the Valley, the Army was only observing the situation there with focus on guarding the LOC and maintenance of communication lines. Initially neither were as many troops available nor was adequate training to handle violent and serious internal threat situations like in the Kashmir Valley. However, the Army had prior experience of counter insurgency operations in the North Eastern states of Nagaland and Mizoram and in Punjab. The situation in the Valley was in no way similar to the ones in the aforementioned states considering the dimension of external and internal support in terms of training , supply of arms and ammunition, manpower and other logistics that the insurgents /militants received.

Additional troops had to be inducted after imparting special Counter Insurgency (CI)/ Counter Terrorism (CT) training to deal with highly motivated pro-Azaadi and pro-Pak militants well amalgamated in the population and urban centres especially in Srinagar and areas north of it. Towards this end the Rashtriya Rifles was also raised later in 1993 to exclusively fight insurgency in J&K. This force was able to relieve the regular troops from CI Operations in which the latter was involved till then, besides deployment along the LOC.

The Army had to be called in to primarily establish law and order and in aid to the civil administration. In doing so it was imperative on the part of the Army to first strictly impose curfew and then carry out search operations in and around population centres, identify and weed out terrorist and anti-national elements from the midst of the masses and establish domination. Its role was also to check infiltration of trained militants along the LOC, carrying out ambushes outside city centres, laying cordon and search operations in peripheral areas etc.

Since the adversary (here own countrymen) fighting an unconventional war had the advantage of jelling into the crowd and had the sympathies of the masses, the task of the Army had been rendered doubly difficult. Door to door searches had to be conducted which could have caused inconveniences and hardship to people. There could have been instances when a few excesses may have been committed during search operations.

During the initial years of the deployment in J&K, the Army had to supercede its normal functioning and undertake the additional responsibility of maintaining civil law and order, a matter otherwise in the hands of the state police force. It is well known that in those years the state police forces and the state administrative machinery had totally collapsed.

To aid the soldier in carrying out these flushing and policing operations certain special powers and legal immunities had to be provided, not only in his personal or his organisation's interest but for the sake of our nation. Thus, the Armed Forces Special Powers (J&K) Act, 1990 had to be promulgated and extended to J&K.

The Eye of Storm – AFSPA

The disturbing violent situation in the North Eastern states particularly in Assam and Manipur prompted the Union Government to first enact the Armed Forces Special Powers Act on 11 Sep 1958. Deemed necessary to provide certain special powers and safeguards to the Armed Forces in a state of deployment to establish normalcy and stability in the insurgency affected region, the Act was gradually extended to other states of the region. It is currently applicable in Assam, Manipur, Nagaland, Mizoram, Tripura, Arunachal Pradesh and Meghalaya.

Considering the situation that had emerged in the state of J&K by 1989-90, the Union Govt by an Act of Parliament, passed the Armed Forces (Jammu and Kashmir) Special Powers Act 1990. It empowered the Armed Forces to deal with an extraordinary circumstance prevailing in the state.

The Act came into effect on 5 July 1990. (Refer to Annexure 2 for details). The Act necessitates the satisfaction of the Governor of the state or the Central Government to declare the whole or any part of the state as 'disturbed' to enforce the (same) Act and thereby vests powers on the Armed Forces to operate in aid of the civil power. Thus, initially the districts of Anantnag, Baramulla, Budgam, Kupwara, Pulwama and Srinagar besides areas falling within 20 kms of the LOC in Rajauri and Poonch were declared as 'disturbed'. By the year 2001, the districts of Jammu, Kathua, Udhampur, Poonch, Rajauri and Doda were also declared 'disturbed' and the AFSPA extended to all of the above.

Translated into ordinary language the most important and overarching sections of the AFSP (J&K) Act 1990 are sections 4,5,6 and 7.

Section 4 It empowers any person of the Armed Forces to search premises and make arrests without warrants. It enables such persons to use force even to the extent of causing death, destroy arms and ammunition dumps, fortifications, shelters etc and also search and seize vehicles. On a closer look Section 4(e) of the Act which empowers the Armed Forces to search and seize weapons is clearly categorized and pronounced in AFSP (J&K) Act than AFSPA 1958.

Section 5 This section is completely new in comparison to the 1958 Act, in that it enables personnel of the Armed Forces to break open and door, almirah, safe etc if the key to any of the mentioned objects is withheld.

Section 6 What we have as Section 6 in the AFSP (J&K) Act is what forms Section 5 of the predecessor Act of 1958. This section of the Act states that arrested persons and seized property is to be made over to the police with the least possible delay. This least possible delay in today's parlance stands at within 48 hours. (Shahbano vs Union of India).

Section 7 This section provides protection of personnel acting in good faith under this Act. Prosecution of any such personnel is granted only with the previous sanction of the Central Government.

Human Rights enthusiasts, militant organisations and a few of the general masses have always had a grudge against the Armed Forces Special Powers Act be it the 1958 or the 1990 versions of it. The sore of their eyes being primarily the implications of the aforementioned sections and provisions of the Act. Little is known about those people's feelings whose lives have been saved or protected because of the Act being in play. No militant or terrorist who must have taken a few lives himself in the name of his holy cause, raped and brutally mutilated women or simply may have taken to the luxury of the powers that the gun can bring to him; wants to be held , tried or even put to death by the state or its forces. No Human Rights activist (self proclaimed guardians of freedom, democracy and the like) wants to be unnoticed siding with those who do not make news. To such people the 'state' is always wrong and they are always right, people who run the state are always as good as fools whereas they, the most learned in the nuances of running the state. Human Rights organisations have often alleged that the AFSPA is violative of Part III of the Indian Constitution especially of Articles 14, 19 and 21 of the sections dealing with fundamental rights of Indian citizens.

In its landmark judgement in the case of Naga Peoples Movement of Human Rights vs the Union of India, the Supreme Court has upheld that the AFSPA is no fraud on the Constitution or a colourful legislation. The Apex Court considered that the conferring of powers on Armed Forces vide Section 4 of AFSPA could not be held arbitrary or violative of Articles 14, 19 and 21 of the Constitution. In fact the Court extended the scope of powers vested vide sections 4 and 6 of the AFSPA so as to include by implication, the power to interrogate the arrested person. It also allowed the Armed Forces to retain the weapons seized during the operations in their own custody rather than hand the seizure over to the police.

The fact that the AFSPA has to be invoked in any geographical area implies that the law and order situation in that particular area has degenerated to an extent that the state government finds itself unable to deal with all its security and legislative agencies. It is to be understood that the Armed Forces do not operate in internal disturbances unless called to do so by the state government. It is virtually impossible for the Armed Forces to operate in aid of the civil authorities without any kind of legal immunity. This legal cover is provided by the AFSPA which in no way allows the Armed Forces to act with impunity.

Strictly speaking, the AFSPA does not provide any new or extraordinary powers to the Armed Forces that is not provided to the state police. A perusal of the various powers available to the police authorities vide provisions of the Criminal Procedure Code (CrPC) vis-à-vis those available to Armed Forces under Sec 4 & 6 AFSPA reveals that the police authorities enjoy more encompassing and wider powers relating to arrest, search, seizure, summoning of witnesses, preventive detention etc, than the Armed Forces.

The immunity provided to Armed Forces personnel vide Sec 7 of the AFSPA is not unique to them alone, in that Section 45 of the CrPC disallows arrest of public servants and Sec 197 provides immunity against prosecution when acting towards the maintenance of law and order. It is compulsory, vide Supreme Court directives, to attain a Govt sanction prior to initiating prosecution against police personnel for excesses of killings committed during the maintenance of law and order. However, Section 45 of the CrPC is not applicable in the state of J&K where Ranbir Penal Code (RPC) is applicable and therefore personnel of Armed Forces can be arrested for any perceived excesses. Prosecution of such individual/s would still require prior sanction of the Central Government.

In keeping with the sprit of Rights guaranteed by the Constitution, the Supreme Court has observed that the instructions issued by the military authorities in the form of the DO's and Don'ts while acting under the AFSPA are to be treated as binding upon all members operating under the circumstances. In a democratic Republic like ours, it is not possible for the Armed Forces to assume sweeping powers and the checks and balances inbuilt in the AFSPA prevent the Armed Forces to do so when acting in aid to the administration. Violation of the provisions of the AFSPA is liable to invite legal action against individuals. Having found the approval of the Supreme Court , the Do's and Don'ts have acquired the status of a law and are absolutely binding on the troops. The said Do's and Don'ts are restrictive in nature and taken very seriously by the Armed Forces in counter insurgency / militancy situations. Prompt disciplinary action is initiated under the Army Act 1950 against any individual not adhering to them.

The Armed Forces deployed in a state in aid to civil powers are legally and constitutionally bound to operate in cooperation with the civil administration to deal with a situation affecting maintenance of public order and law which necessitates the deployment in the first place so that normalcy is restored. The Government still remains at the helm of affairs in matters of governance which is not and cannot be taken over by the Armed Forces. Though a cursory look at the bare Act implies to many to give sweeping powers to the Armed Forces, but noteworthy is the fact that these powers are also vested on the local police force even in the absence of deployment of troops. Perhaps the powers vested in the police are more extended, in that it has the power to investigate the offences too. It would thus not be totally incorrect to say that the AFSPA grants policing powers to the Armed Forces deployed in counter insurgency / militancy situations.

One may argue that the very concept of AFSPA is rights and freedom restrictive but it is to be understood that when circumstances demand, individual rights may have to be curbed or derogated for the greater rights of the society. Individual freedom has to be balanced with the freedom of other individuals living in society and the state. It is the duty of the state to do the balancing act.

Though the Constitution of India guarantees individual citizens certain Fundamental Rights, it also beholdens the Government to protect every state not only from external aggression but also internal disturbances (Art 355) and to ensure that the governance of every state is carried out in accordance with the provisions of the Constitution.

On further analysis of section 7 of the AFSPA one may clearly derive that the protection guaranteed by the same is only for those duties and not in any kind of malice of the duties and responsibilities . Section 7 reads : "Protection of persons acting in good faith under this Act. No prosecution, suit or other legal proceeding shall be instituted , except with the previous sanction of the Central Government, against any person in respect of anything done or purported to be done in exercise of the powers conferred by this Act". Thus the protection is not available to any such personnel who may commit a criminal offence not in the discharge of his official duty even in an area which is declared disturbed.

It has to be understood that personnel of the Armed Forces acting under the AFSPA are accountable for all their actions and cannot act with impunity. The AFSPA does not allow the Armed Forces to assume sweeping powers. The Act along with the Do's and Don'ts are a guide to their operational functionality in a hostile domestic situation and they are not sans the human aspects. The AFSPA is a 'law' (ref: Conversation with Shri N.N. Vohra, Governor, J&K, 31 May 2010) which enables the Armed Forces to carry out operations with legal immunity, the same that is provided to any state police force.

5

Cautions - The Do's and the Don'ts

Protection and respect of human dignity, human decency and human rights are the very essence of the rule of law and social order in any civilised society. Armed Forces are called in aid to civil authorities to maintain law and order as also to provide assistance in case of natural disasters and catastrophes. Thus members of the Armed Forces act as the protectors of the social order so that other citizens can enjoy the fruits in an orderly society.

When deployed in aid to civil authority, the Armed Forces of the country operate in the state concerned in cooperation with the civil administration so that the situation affecting maintenance of public order, which has necessitated the deployment of the Armed Forces, is effectively dealt with and normalcy is restored. The Armed Forces Special Powers Act does not displace the civil power of the state by the Armed Forces. It only provides for special powers and legal immunity to the Armed Forces deployed to deal with a situation which the civil power finds itself unable to tackle.

The Do's and Don'ts are binding instructions which are required to be followed by the members of the Armed Forces exercising power under Armed Forces Special Powers Act and any disregard of these instructions entails suitable action under the Army Act 1950.

The DO's While in Action

Translated into mandatory cautions to be exercised by the Armed Forces, the AFSPA does not appear to be as sweeping and threatening as is generally perceived.

The Dos as have been interpreted in military parlance by the Force Commanders clearly categorise CI action into three parts viz action before operation, action during operation and action after operation. **Action before operation** makes it mandatory for troops to operate in the area declared 'disturbed' under Section 3 of the AFSPA. It lists that before opening fire or using force it is to be ensured that prohibitory orders against the assembly of 5 or more persons or carrying of weapons on fire arms / ammunition or explosive substance exists in the area declared 'disturbed' and the persons concerned have acted in contravention of such order.

The power to open fire or arrest is vested only upon an officer / Junior Commissioned Officer (JCO), Warrant Officer (WO) or a Non-commissioned Officer (NCO) who shall do so only when satisfied that such an action is necessary for maintenance of public order and after giving due warning to the opponent, vide Section 4 of the AFSPA (J&K) Act.

Vide Section 4(b) any Officer, JCO, WO and NCO is empowered to destroy those arms dump, prepared or fortified position or shelter from which armed attacks are made or are likely to be made or any structure used as training camp for armed militants or utilised as hide-out by armed militants or absconders wanted for any offence, provided prior to taking such action such officer is of the opinion that it is necessary to destroy any arms dump etc.

Powers have been conferred under Section 4(a) of the AFSPA to arrest any person without warrant. This may appear to be sweeping, unconstitutional and rights restrictive at the initial glance and may have also led to certain disappearances as has been alleged over the years. However, if followed and applied in true spirit such a power can only be exercised if that person has committed cognisable offence or against whom there lies reasonable suspicion that he has committed cognisable offence or is about to commit a cognisable offence. For effecting arrest such force as may be necessary can be exercised. More so, it has to be ensured that only such a person who has either committed a cognisable offence or against whom reasonable suspicion exists, is arrested. Innocent persons are not to be arrested.

Under Section 4(d) of the AFSPA, power can be exercised to enter and search without warrant any premises, to make any such arrest of any person as mentioned in sub-para 4(b) to recover any person believed to be wrongfully restrained or confined or any property reasonably suspected to be stolen property or any arms, ammunition or explosive substances believed to be unlawfully kept in such premises and the concerned person may for that purpose use such force as may be necessary. Before launching any such raid / search, definite information about the activity is obtained from the local source and or civil authorities. Lastly, it is to be ensured that the troops deployed in aid to civil authorities operate in the state concerned in cooperation with the civil administration.

Action during operation pertaining use of force: It is imperative that while exercising powers conferred under Section 4 of AFSPA, minimal force required for effective action against the person / persons acting in contravention is to be used. If there is a necessity to open fire or use any force against any person/s, it is to be ascertained that the same is essential for maintenance of public order and applied only after giving due warning.

While on a search mission, the concerned persons about to make a search are to ensure that two or more independent and respected members of the society / community are available to be a witness to the process, to attend and witness the search and may issue an order in writing to them. The search is to be made in their presence and a list of all things seized in the course of such search and of the places in which they are respectively found is to be prepared by such officer or other person and signed by such witnesses. However, no person witnessing a search under this section is required to be present at court as a witness of the search unless specially summoned by it.

During any search of a dwelling place, an occupant of such a place or some person on his behalf should be permitted to attend the search and a copy of the list duly signed by the said witnesses is to be given to such an occupant or person.

While making a search of a woman or effecting the arrest of a woman or while searching any premise in occupation of a woman, any person operating under the Act has to follow the procedure meant for a police officer as contemplated under the various provisions of the CrPC, viz, the provision to sub section (2) section 47, sub-section (2) of section 51, sub-section (3) of section 106 and the provision of sub-section (1) of section 160 of CrPC.

It is to be ensured by Commanders that troops under their command do not harass innocent people, destroy property of the public or unnecessarily enter into house of people not connected with any unlawful activity.

Lastly it is to be ensured that proper record is maintained of the arrested and released person after apprehension.

Directives are that a list of the arrested persons be prepared and the arrested be handed over the officer-in-charge of the nearest police station with least possible delay along with a report of the circumstances causing the arrest so that the arrested person can be produced before the nearest Magistrate within 24 hours of his arrest excluding the time taken for travelling from the place of arrest to the court of the magistrate. Further every delay in handing over such an arrested person to the police must be justified depending upon the place, time of arrest and the territory in which such person had been arrested.

List of all property; arms, ammunition or any other incriminating material / documents taken into possession after a raid is an absolute necessity as also handing the same over to the officer-in-charge of the nearest police station together with a report of the circumstances leading to such a search and seizure.

After the handing over of any such arrested person/s or property stores etc., a receipt of the same needs to be obtained from the police and a record maintained of all such receipts.

The maintenance of record of the personnel (officers and troops) forming such task forces as also of the area where operations are launched with other details of date, time etc is made an absolute must.

It is directed that medical relief to all persons injured during an encounter is ensured. In the event of any fatal casualty, the dead body is to be handed over immediately to the officer-in-charge of the nearest police station along with the details leading to the death of the person concerned. A detailed record of the entire operation is to be maintained in all its correctness and explicitly.

Following from the detailed list of 'Do's are the 'Don'ts which guide troops in operation in counter insurgency and militancy in Jammu and Kashmir as they do in the North East. The carefully thought out provisions to be followed and carried out by each and every person operating in J&K avoid coming in the way of law and diluting the very purpose of the deployment.

Of foremost importance is the provision that no person under custody is to be held for any period longer than the bare necessity for handing over to the nearest police station.

In keeping with international standards, the use of third degree methods to extract information or confession for involvement in unlawful activities is strictly prohibited. Instructions are clear about the use of force as no force is to be applied on any arrested person except when he is trying to escape.

No arrested person can be released directly after the apprehension. The release of such person/s is to be affected only through the civil police. Any such arrested person is not to be taken after he is handed over to the police.

Nobody is permitted to tamper with official records.

The Ten Commandments as Issued by the Chief of the Army Staff (CrPC 130-131)

Translating the legal language into colloquial dictates for troops in J&K, the Commanders of the Armed Forces have issued Do's & Don'ts in the form of what has come to be known as the 'Ten Commandments of the Chief of Army Staff' (COAS).

The following are what the troops are required to 'Do' while in any operation

(a) Act in close cooperation with civil authorities throughout.

(b) Maintain inter communication if possible by telephone / radio.

(c) Obtain requisition from the Magistrate when present.

(d) Use as little force and do as little injury to person and property as may be consistent with attainment of objective in view.

(e) In case you decide to open fire –

    (i) Give warning in local language that fire will be effective.

    (ii) Attract attention before firing by bugle or other means.

    (iii) Distribute your men in fire units with specified Commanders.

    (iv) Control fire by issuing personal orders.

    (v) Note number of rounds fired.

    (vi) Aim at the front of the crowd actually rioting or inciting to riot or at conspicuous ring leaders ie, do not fire into the thick of the crowd at the back.

    (vii) Aim low and shoot for effect with personal weapons on specific orders.

    (viii) Ceasefire immediately once the object has been attained.

    (ix) Take steps to secure wounded.

    (x) Maintain cordial relations with civilian authorities and Para-military Force.

    (xi) Ensure high standards of discipline.

The Don'ts are as :-

(a) Do not use excessive force.

(b) Do not get involved in hand struggle with mob.

(c) Do not ill-treat any one, in particular women and children.

(d) Do not harass any civilian.

(e) Do not resort to any torture.

(f) Do not show any communal bias while dealing with civilians.

(g) Do not meddle in civilian administration affairs.

(h) Do not accept loss/surrender of weapons by troops.

(j) Do not accept presents, donations and rewards.

(k) Do not resort to indiscriminate firing.

Existing Laws, Rights, Paradigm

Considering the fact that the AFSPA and the Armed Forces have ever been in the eye of the storm and have faced vehement as well as violent protests from general populace especially from rights groups, it becomes imperative to learn of the same rights and international standards which enthusiasts allege the aforementioned subjects violate.

The preceding sections/ paragraph aimed to interpret the AFSPA and the consequential Do's and Don'ts as dictates binding on troops, necessitating an analysis or a study on whether any of the provisions are in contravention of any international law or standard or in contravention of the Indian Constitution. For this purpose one must list the UN Charter and the Universal Declaration of Human Rights (UDHR).

(i) All human beings are born free and equal in dignity and rights (UN Charter and UDHR).

(ii) No one shall be subjected to arbitrary arrest, detention or exile.

(iii) No person shall be subjected to unlawful and prolonged detention.

(iv) Everyone has the right to life, liberty and security of person .

(v) No one shall be subjected to torture or to cruel, inhuman or degrading treatment or punishment.

(vi)   Everyone has the right to well being of himself and his family. On humanitarian grounds, medical help and care have to be pro vided to sick and wounded of even an enemy as laid down in the Geneva Conventions.

(vii) Everyone has the right to freedom of movement and residence within the border of each state.

(viii) Every one has the right to own property alone as well as in asso ciation with others. No one shall be arbitrarily deprived of his property.

(ix)   All are equal before law and are entitled without any discrimi nation to equal protection of law. Everyone is entitled to the universal protection of human rights without distinction of any kind, such as race, colour, sex, language, religion, political or other opinion national or social origin, property, birth or other status.

(x)   No one shall be subjected to arbitrary interference with his pri vacy, family, home, or correspondence nor attack upon his honour or reputation.

(xi)   Everyone has the right to freedom of thought, conscience and religion. This right includes freedom to change his religion or belief and freedom either alone or in community with others and in public or private, to manifest his religion or belief in teaching, practice, worship and observance.

(xii) Everyone has the right to freedom of speech and expression. This right includes freedom to hold opinion without interference, to seek, receive and impart information and ideas through any me dia and regardless of frontiers.

Human Rights may be defined from various angles such as individual, collective, civil, social, economic, religious and so on to every realm of human existence and human activity. As regards a single definition of the term, the definition given in the Protection of Human Rights Act 1993 is the most exhaustive. Section 2 (d) of the Act defines human rights as under :-

> "Human Rights mean the rights relating to life, liberty, equality and dignity of the individual guaranteed by the Constitution or embodied in the international covenants and enforceable by courts in India". (Refer to Annexure 3)

The words 'Human Rights' do not find mention anywhere in the Indian Constitution but Part III of the Constitution which deals with the Fundamental Rights is almost a complete charter of Human Rights. It includes rights like equality before law, equality of opportunity in matters of employment, prevention of discrimination on grounds of race, sex, caste, religion, freedom of speech and expressions, rights to freedom or religion, right to freedom of movement, cultural and educational rights, right to constitutional remedies, to list a few.

Moreover, the Universal Declaration of Human Rights, International Covenant on Civil and Political Rights (ICCPR), International Covenant on Social, Economic and Cultural Rights and the two Optional Protocols to the ICCPR and other treaties have widened the definition and scope of human rights. These include human dignity, personal freedom, equality of opportunity in matters of employment, protection of privacy, the rights not to be subjected to torture or other cruel, inhuman or degrading treatment or punishment, prohibition of discrimination on ground of race, caste, colour, sex, language, religion, political and other opinion, national or social origin, property, birth or status, freedom of speech and expression, freedom to assemble peacefully, freedom to form associations and unions, freedom to move freely, freedom to reside anywhere, right to development, protection against death, penalty, protection to refugees and many more such rights. Thus human rights include all civil, political, economic, social and cultural rights as enshrined in various international documents.

Human Rights enshrined in the Universal Declaration of Human Rights was adopted by the United Nations General Assembly on the 10th December 1948.

Article 1 of the Declaration states that "all human beings are born free and equal in dignity and rights". The Human Rights are the same for all regardless of their origin, sex, domicile, wealth, religion or any other factor. Human rights are inherent and inalienable rights of every human being. However, they cannot be brought to mean the rights of the individual only. The promotion of collective Human Rights, applying to groups or classes of people is also of practical significance.

In this context a definition of Legal, Natural and Fundamental rights may also be provided for anyone to understand the differences or commonalities between the same and the concept of human rights.

Legal rights are those rights of an individual which are the creation of statutes and the remedy for their violation lies in the remedy laid down in the relevant statute. It may be imprisonment or compensation.

Natural rights are quite close to human rights and are those rights which naturally flow to a person by virtue of being born a human. These rights have been in existence even before the birth of a political society. These are inviolable rights.

Fundamental rights in the Indian context are those rights that are enshrined in Part III of the Indian Constitution. They are inviolable and enforceable by the courts by way of writs, orders and direction. Since the Fundamental Rights do not cover all aspects of Human Rights, the founders of the Constitution have incorporated certain principles which are fundamental in the governance of the country in the form of Directive Principles of State Policy into the Constitution. The Indian judiciary has been interpreting the Fundamental Rights and the Directive Principles of State Policy in tune with the international Human Rights from time to time.

While some of the rights enlisted in Part III may be enjoyed by Indian citizens there are others which are enjoyed by all persons living within the Indian territory.

Clause 2 of Article 13 lays that the state shall not make any law which takes away or abridges the rights conferred by Part III and any law made in contravention of this clause shall to the extent of this contravention, be void. But the 24th Amendment Act 1971 lays down that Fundamental Rights can be amended by Parliament by amending the Constitution under Article 368.

The Constitution has also made provision for making these rights effective by providing for certain judicial remedies. The Constitution however has authorised the state directly to impose certain limitations upon Fundamental

Rights. Thus in India, the rights have not been formulated in absolute terms. In times of national emergency, the rights may be suspended by the state.

To illustrate at least one of such 'rights' and its limitations we may consider the right to freedom.

The right to freedom has been recognised by the provision of Articles 19-22 of the Constitution. Article 19 deals with six items of freedom and their limitation. Article 20-22 elaborately describe personal freedom.

The first of the six freedoms laid down in Article 19 is –

(a) Right to freedom of speech and expression : A restrain lies in the exercise of this right which was imposed by the Constitution (First Amendment) Act 1951. The Constitution provides that the Parliament may make laws imposing reasonable restriction on the exercise of this right in the interest of the sovereignty and integrity of India, the security of the state, friendly relation with foreign states, public order, decency or morality or in relation to contempt of court, defamation or incitement to an offence.

(b) Right to assemble peacefully and without arms : Section 3 of Article 19 also lays down that the right may be restricted on reasonable grounds. The reasonableness of the restriction can be determined by Courts only.

(c) Right to form associations or unions : Though this provision gives the right to form trade unions, political parties, youth organisations, scientific organisations and the like, it prohibits the forming of any association for the purpose of committing any offence or for conspiring against the state.

(d) Right to move freely throughout the territory of India : This right too may be curtailed on reasonable grounds viz, security of the state.

(e) Right to reside and settle in any part of the territory of India.

(f) Right to practice any profession or to carry on ay occupation, trade or business.

The above two items are not without limitations either. Personal freedom enlisted in Articles 20-22 of the Constitution too are not without their limitations.

It is important to remember here that Human Rights in the Indian context are those rights which are defined in the National Human Rights Act or other statutes.

We have here to agree with the honourable Supreme Court of India in its land mark judgement on the Naga Peoples Movement for Human Rights vs the Union of India that the AFSPA is no fraud on the Constitution nor is the conferring of powers to the Armed Force violative of certain Fundamental Rights

A few still argue that the powers vested on Armed Forces to arrest without warrant is in contravention with the right of individuals not to be subjected to arbitrary arrest, detention or exile but the nuance lies in the fact that a personnel can do so only when he is satisfied that the person has committed cognisable offence or against whom there lies reasonable suspicion that he has committed so or is about to commit a cognisable offence.

So far as arbitrary detention is concerned, even while operating under AFSPA the detainee has to be handed over to the nearest police station with least possible delay so that the arrested person can be produced before the nearest Magistrate within 24 hours.

The AFSPA as well as the 'Commandments' prohibit the use of torture or inhuman treatment to extract information or otherwise.

We have seen earlier that directives are also to provide medical relief to all persons injured during an encounter.

Directives are clear on each and every operational move while countering insurgency / militancy and adequate measures taken not to violate any right of the individual. If however, violations do occur, any individual/ s can seek judicial remedy and the erring personnel/s be brought to justice.

6 Some Ground Realities

Through the twenty plus years that militancy has passed from one phase to the other in Kashmir, it needs well to be understood that it is the Kashmiri people who have suffered the most . Estimates put more than 47,234 reported incidences of terrorist violence since 1988. According to the official figures released in 2009 by the Ministry of Indian Health and Family Welfare 14,808 Muslims, 1748 Hindus and 115 Sikhs were killed in this reign of militancy in Kashmir since 1989. Thousands have been injured and maimed. Not only killings, the politics of militancy and perhaps an ethnic cleansing has caused the displacement of thousands of Kashmiri Pundits (rough estimate puts it at 1,70,000 to 7,00,000) right at the onset.

Another uncomfortable fact that has emerged in this milieu is that of disappearances of people. As stated earlier (Chapter III), unemployment, lack of developmental activities coupled with mal-administration led to disillusionment and frustration amongst the youth. Batches of youngsters had crossed over to POK and Pakistan to be indoctrinated and trained in arms and explosives handling. These batches were then sent back to Kashmir to wage a Holy War against the government and its security apparatus. We have also seen earlier that the ideologies of the militant organisations which harboured the armed militants vary from Jihad - to independence for Kashmir - to a merger with Pakistan. Of course, initially they received wide support from the local population. Though much of the financial and arms and ammunition support came from across the border (which continues even to this day), moral, ideological and logistic support was to be found in abundance from the local population. Thus emerged another non combatant genre of people who are known as Over Ground Workers (OGWs).

These OGWs work as guides, intelligence gatherers, feelers and also provide for the militants' logistic support. They continue to be the militants support system in carrying out the missions assigned to them by their masters.

Legally speaking the OGWs are as accountable in the conflict in abetment and carrying out of a war as the armed militant themselves.

Thus logically it can be understood that when the state began cracking down on the armed combatants ripples of it would have affected the OGWs too.

Views expressed in this section are a collection from various sections of the Kashmir society. For a clear perspective it may be divided into three distinct categories :-

(a)   That of the Civil Society.

(b)   That of the state machinery.

(c)   That of the ordinary people

(a) Civil Society's Take on the Army/Security Forces.

Kashmir centric Human Rights and Civil Societies believe that the Army, the Police and other security agencies systematically carry out violation of Human Rights often resorting to extra-judicial , summary and arbitrary killing, besides other methods of torture.

Reports of Human Rights violations pertaining particularly to disappearances put the figures anywhere from 8000 to 10000 since 1989.[1] Officially the Minister for Parliamentary Affairs though admitted in the Legislative Assembly in 2003 that a total of 3931 persons had disappeared since the beginning of militancy in Kashmir. Of the numbers disappeared he attributed maximum from the districts of Kupwara and Baramulla (761 and 852 respectively) (This can be co-related to the fact of maximum numbers of local terrorists being recruited by JKLF and the like from the

---

[1] According to an article by Praveena Ahangar, www.ahrck.net/ua/main, afad-online.org, www.ielrc.org, www.hrw.org/campaigns/kashmir/Indiarole

said places round that time as also of constitution of the other Tanzeems).

To assign 8000 to 10000 cases of disappearances as cases of violation caused by Armed Forces alone seems utterly hypothetical and without any merit.

Further to this, the International People's Tribunal on Human Rights and Justice in Indian Administered Kashmir (IPTK) which claims to have investigated sites of mass burials or mass graves, in its report titled 'Buried Evidence' states that the graveyards investigated entomb bodies of those murdered in encounter and fake killings between 1990-09. They claim that the graves include bodies of extra-judicial, summary and arbitrary executions as well as massacres committed by the Indian military and para-military forces. According to the same report, 2373 graves (87.9%) were unnamed. Of these graves, 154 contained two bodies each and 23 contained more than two cadavers. The report alleges that the graves in Bandipora, Baramulla and Kupwara are a part of a 'collective burial' by India's military, and para-military creating a 'landscape of mass burial' . These graveyards have been termed as 'secret graveyards' where bodies are claimed to have been brought by the Police, being last in the chain of handlers.

This organisation believes that if independent investigations were to be undertaken in all the ten districts of the Valley, then it would be reasonable to assume that the 8000 plus 'enforced' disappearances since 1989 would correlate with the number of bodies in unknown, unmarked and mass graves.

Going by the book 'Did they Vanish in Thin Air?' by Mr Zahir-ud-din there were at least 115 cases of enforced disappearances during the period 1993-2001. The author of the aforementioned book has independently researched each of the cases and has categorically named Army/ RR Units, BSF and CRPF battalions responsible for the disappearances.

It appears in many cases of killings and disappearances that the Police has not and does not register FIRs which is perhaps the first step to any formal enquiry being conducted.

Organisations like the IPTK, Jammu and Kashmir Coalition of Civil Society (JKCCS) and their like within the state and outside squarely believe that the Armed Forces operate with impunity. Reports such as 'Buried Evidence', 'Peace and Process of Violence' , 'Militarisation with Impunity',

'Dead but not forgotten' are rife with anti-army / SF and anti-establishment sentiments.

The JKCCS believes that the Army is an occupational force doing the dirty job of the Government of India, owing 'allegiance to the state and not to the people'. The Army's orientation they opine, is to follow orders and whatever it does reflects what orders it has got from the Government of India.

Needless to say that civil societies such as these want the AFSPA repealed and the Army / SF back in their barracks. On a softer note, they take pity on soldiers living far away from their families and facing the hatred of the people of Kashmir.

According to a spokesperson of JKCCS (Mr Khurram Pervez) what angers the people of Kashmir is New Delhi's unwillingness to allow a democratic referendum on the Kashmir Issue. Adding to this he iterated that all New Delhi does is flex its muscle power in Kashmir through its security agencies, thus choking the political space of the people. As per the spokesperson, the people of Kashmir are very clear about 'self determination'. Though there is no denial that a section of the population wants a merger with Pakistan, a vast majority wants independence . On the other hand, he opined that political parties such as the National Conference and the PDP contend for greater autonomy for the state of J&K.

Misinformation prevails amongst a section of the society (or is deliberately spread) that the Centre is in control over the natural resources of Kashmir. The people, it was opined, should be in control of their land and its resources.

According to the spokesperson, the people of Kashmir have never been able to identify themselves as Indians and fail to do so even now. The divide, it was claimed, is even wider now. To them the 'Indian Government' is a hegemon and its hegemony is manifested by its Army and other security agencies which is exemplified by the presence of approx. 7 (seven) lakh troops (as per the spokesperson's estimates) to counter 700 militants in the Valley.

(b) Presence and of International Committee of the Red Cross (ICRC) in Jammu and Kashmir.

The presence of the ICRC in J & K is significant in that it underlines that there is an armed conflict situation prevailing in the state no matter how peaceful enthusiasts claim the dissent to be. Being an international community, its perception of the role of the Armed Forces and other security agencies matter much to the international community and the Government agencies. (However, no comment was made to the author on the working of the Armed Forces).

The ICRC's role in J&K is mainly to visit places of detention and arrested persons in connection to the situation prevailing in the state. It tasks itself in monitoring the treatment given to detainees and their conditions of detention. The findings of such visits is shared confidentially with authorities. Information taken during private interactions with detainees during such visits may be used in reports submitted to Indian authorities with the permission of the detainee only. The ICRC helps detainees and their families to establish and maintain contact.

Besides, the ICRC promotes the spread of International Humanitarian Law to various sections of the society. It supports the Indian Red Cross Society in running rehabilitation centres and providing free treatment to the patients, conducting First Aid courses, training volunteers in security and disaster response activities while operating in dangerous / difficult situations. It also supports the ICRC in raising awareness about its unique role as an independent and impartial humanitarian organisation

(c) The State Machinery's Take on the AFSPA VIS-A-VIS the Army

The deployment of the Army in J&K to contain militancy / insurgency and in aid to the civil administration vested on the soldiers conflicting military and national laws and tenets of basic training.

Whereas the Army is trained to fight a regular conflict, it now had to deal with unseen, undistinguishable enemy within populated areas. And as the situation prevailed in the late 80s and through the 1990s in J&K, discerning friend from foe was an uphill task. This is especially so because public sentiments were with the insurgents and intelligence hard to come.

Collapse of the state machinery led to the declaration of Governor's Rule bringing thus the state under the Centre's string pull till election could be next held.

The Armed Forces as is common knowledge, is a subject matter of the Central Government. Through relentless efforts to restore normalcy, elections were conducted and a state government set in place. And here set in another conflicting area of control, command and accountability over and of the Army.

In matters of Kashmir which ever political party may come to power would have its own stake on AFSPA and the presence of the Army in the state, based on its own ideologies. But there appears to be the basic understanding that the AFSPA as a 'legal framework' which is 'required' (ref: Conversation with Shri Omar Abdullah, CM, J&K, June 2, 2010) for the Armed Forces to operate if at all it is to operate in the state.

The eye sores in AFSPA are sections 4,5, 6 and 7 which allow personnel (of a certain level) to open fire, search and frisk. The fact that prosecution of personnel (acting under AFSPA) is difficult without prior Central Government sanction, makes it a questionable law to many. Political parties and separatists have been busing themselves over either repealing the Act or diluting it – making it more 'humane' (ref: Conversation with Shri Omar Abdullah, CM, J&K, June 2, 2010). The view (as expressed by the Governor, J&K, His Excellency Shri NN Vohra, May 31, 2010 and Shri Omar Abdullah, CM, J&K, June 2, 2010) that the Army can operate without the 'immunisation' of the AFSPA as a protective cover to the State Police or as the Police functions sans the Act, puts into question the very role played by the Army in countering militancy in the state. For the Army to provide just a protective cover to the Police implies that the State Police has to take the lead in combating militancy. The current practice is that of joint operation with the Army in the lead.

Here again it has to be gauged whether the State Police is equipped in terms of training, motivation (given the fact that State Police personnel are recruited largely from the local population and are often under pressure of the militants) and manpower to take the lead in the combat against militancy and Proxy War. In case the State Police force is ready for all the above then there is no need for the Army's engagement even as a 'protective cover' (ref: Conversation with the Governor , J&K, Shri NN Vohra, May 31, 2010). The Army's presence would merely be auxiliary and overlapping.

Another problem area is the state's jurisdictional limit over the Army. The Army being a Central force does not come under the investigative purview of the State Human Rights Commission nor under the National Human Rights Commission (NHRC).[2] Cases of alleged Human Rights Violation which are dealt with by the Army are allegedly 'never made public' which 'creates distrust' (ref: Conversation with Shri Omar Abdullah, CM , J&K, June 2, 2010) of the people in the Army and its procedures. This lack of the 'element of transparency' (ref: Conversation with Shri Omar Abdullah, CM, J&K; June 2, 2010) distances the already suspicious people from the Army.

It would be utopian to assume that there could have been no instances of Human Rights violations at all by troops in an exigent situation over such extended period of time. There may have been infringements and high handed behavior by troops in the initial stages of deployment.[3]

There have been isolated cases[4] of violation and adequate punishment has been metted out to the guilty. But a negative publicity of such cases and of alleged many more such cases in the media (especially the vernacular press) had created an anti-Army sentiment and a propaganda tool in the hands of militant organisations and Human Rights Organisations (HROs) to stall operations.

To bridge the gap between itself and the people as also in aid to the civil administration, the Army had undertaken developmental works in J&K named Operation Sadbhavna.[5] It is to the credit of the Army that the Operation has been highly successful, more so as it has 'progressively' (ref: conversation with Shri NN Vohra, Governor, J&K : May 31, 2010) brought the people closer to the Army especially in remote areas and has

---

[2] See Chapter IX for the role of NHRC.

[3] This can be attributed to the troops training and orientation to fight a regular war. This orientation has undergone a sea-change over the years through constant training and sensitisation in Human Rights.

[4] See Chapter X for details.

[5] See Chapter VIII for details.

helped in changing 'public perception of the Army' (ref: conversation with Shri Omar Abdullah, CM, J&K : June 2, 2010).

The projects under Operation Sadbhavna which are being administratively run by the Army now, are ultimately to be handed over to the civil administration . The Army cannot be expected to 'continue', (ref: Conversation with Shri Omar Abdullah, CM, J&K : June 2, 2010) though many would like, undertaking developmental works with an elected State Government in place.

The relationship of the Army with the people of J&K seems to have a very fine chord attached. On one hand, at the slightest instance, thousands of locals shout anti-Army slogans including voices from political parties, want the Army back in its barracks, while on the other, they would want the Army to 'continue' with its developmental works (ref : Conversation with Shri Omar Abdullah, CM, J&K: June 2, 2010)

Since the chord is delicate and has taken years to tie, the Army needs to be extra cautious in not upsetting the people by committing blunders like Human Rights violations. Incidences such as the alleged encounter killing at Rafiabad (Machil Sector) April 2010, tarnish the image of not as much of the individual perpetrator/s as of the entire institution called the Army. It points a questionable finger at the 'training and conduct' (ref: Conversation with Shri NN Vohra, Governor, J&K; May 31, 2010) of the Army and its personnel and its 'Standard Operating Procedure' (ref: Conversation with Shri NN Vohra, Governor, J&K,

May 31, 2010).   Aberrations like these leave the Government in a difficult position to 'answer the people' (Ref : Conversation with Shri NN Vohra, Governor, J&K, May 31, 2010) and vouch for such functionally required AFSPA and operationally required Army.

The Army after the alleged incidence in a clear stance of 'zero tolerance' initiated its own probe parallel to the Magisterial enquiry ordered by the Chief Minister. In an unprecedented move, the Army had handed over the accused officer to the Police for the law to take its own course. The Army had suspended the accused officer and had taken away command from the CO of the unit.

01 MAY 2010 **3 KILLED IN** **KUPWARA SECTOR** SRINAGAR, April 30. Army today claimed to have killed three milltants while following an Infiltration told in the machill Sector of the line of control (LOC) in kupware district while some millitants managed their escape	**GREATER** **KASHMIR 28** **MAY 2010** **CM ORDERS** **PROBE IN** **MACHIL** **KILLINGS** **PROTEST IN** **RAFIABAD:** **EXHUMATION** **TODAY** Varmul may 27: jammu and Kashmir government Thursday ordered a magisterial Probe into the killing of three youth from Nadinal, Raflabad in an alleged fake encounter... April 30.	**EXHUMATION** **TODAY** Minister of State for Health Javed Ahmed Dar, who is also MLA Raflabad told Greater Kashmir that bodies of the slain youth would be exhumed onFriday "I have brought the matter into the notice of the Chief Minister Omar Abdullah	**2 ACCUSED** **ARRESTED: Police** **Srinagar, May: Jammu** **and Kashmir Police** **have arrested two** **persons in connection** **with the disappearance** **case of the three** **missing youth of Nadihal** **, a police spokesman** **Said, "The arrested** **persons are being** **questioned and a case** **under section 364** **Ranbir Panel Code has** **been registered against** **them,"**
KASHMIR IMAGES **28 MAY 2010** **3 YOUTH KILLED** **IN FAKE** **ENCOUNTER** **Srinagar MAY 27:** Army has allegedly killed three boys of nadihal Baramulla in fake encounter at LOC in Machil Sector of kupware on April 30.	**Kingpin nabbed** **Srinagar, May** **28: police have** **arrested a** **trooper of** **Territorial Army** **Abbes Hussein** **who**	**DAILY EXCEL** **SIOR 29 MAY** **2010: FAKE** **encounter at** **Machil?** **Bodies of 3 Youth** **exhumed 3 held** **Srinagar May 28:** **Authorities today** **exhumed three** **bodies of the** **"militants" killed in** **an "encounter"**	**GREATER KASHMIR** **29 MAY 2010 BODIES** **EXHUMED,** **IDENTIFIED MORE** **SKELETONS** **TUMBLE OUT** Kalaroos (Kupwara), May 28: Amid a Complete shutdown and Pro-freedom protests
MACHILL **KILLINGS: TA** **TROOPER** **ARRESTED, HUNT** **ON FOR MAJOR:** **Police Register** **Abduction Murder** **Case Against Army** **Srinagar, May 28:** **Police have filled a** **case of abduction and** **murder against the** **army for the killing of** **Protests rock** **Raflabad Raflabad,** **May 28: The** **Raflabad township** **observed complete** **shutdown and people** **GOC 15 Corps** **Srinagar, May 28:** **Relterating** **government 's Zero** **tolerance to human** **rights violations, the** **chief minister**		**RISING KASHMIR** **29 MAY 2010 Bar** **to approach HC** **over "fake** **encounter"** Srinagar , May 28: Condemning the killing of three youth in an alleged fake encounter, **3 bodies exhumed at** **Kalaroos Fake** **encounter 2010:** **Raflabad, May 28:** **The bodies of three** **youth of Nadihal** **Raflabad, who were** **killed in fake**	**Machil killings evoke** **widespread** **condemnation Srinagar,** **May 28: The Killing of** **three youth in an** **alleged fake encounter** **by army in Machil** **sector last** **KASHMIR IMAGES** **29 MAY 2010 Police to** **register murder case** **against Major** **Srinagar, May 28:** **Jammu and Kashmir** **Police will register a** **murder case against an** **Army major and**

By taking such steps, the Army has proved how serious and 'more sensitive' it is in matters of Human Rights violation by its men (ref: Conversation with Shri Omar Abdullah, CM, J&K : June 2, 2010).

(C) Voices of the Ordinary People -Their Take on the Army, Administration and Militancy

> **Disclaimer :** A lot of thought went in to formulate this section and the best appeared to give a narrative as gathered from the interactions with locals at Lolab, Trehgam (North Kashmir), Balapur, Anantnag (South Kashmir). For reasons of security and fear of the people, names will rarely be mentioned nor will any one be directly quoted. Views expressed here are strictly that of the people gathered at the meetings braving many fears.

What people in the rest of the country and elsewhere perceive of Kashmir and the Kashmiri people is mostly dominated by media reports and violence shown therein. Stone pelting youths and children, thousands of angry protestors demonstrating and sometimes that of troops taking position are seen and heard in the electronic and print media. The rest of the voices and faces shroud in a veil of mystery, as if not there at all. Other than the voices of Mr Geelaini or the Mirwaiz nothing or very less of the voices of the ordinary people of the Valley manage to cross the Banihal Pass.

The aspirations of the people have been indicated well in the Assembly polls of 2008, the Parliamentary elections of 2009 and very recently the Panchayat elections of 2011.

What follows is an account of the ordinary peoples' take on issues such as militancy, Army's role and presence, security, administration etc. which determine their way of life and living.

Lolab (North Kashmir)

At a gathering of village elders, women and youth, it was learnt that the people in Lolab, Sogam, Devar Lasipora, Tikipora (all in North Kashmir, close to the LOC) were generally afraid of the Army until 2005. This fear they alleged was consequential to the Army's harshness towards them. The Army, they alleged, would often rough people up during search operations. This attitude (the same people counter) has changed ever-since 2005 and as of now they are at ease with the Army's presence in the area.

Addressing people at Lolab

A major inconvenience faced by the people there is their passage through the Zangli gate after 6 pm. According to them transporting patients in need of urgent medical attention also is next to impossible and the procedure to obtain permission is long drawn. These people claimed to have taken up the matter with the Deputy Commissioner who they allege, has done nothing in this regard. They said they have no problems in being thoroughly frisked at the gate during such emergency transits but they must be allowed to pass.

Another inconvenience caused to the people here appeared to be the restriction imposed on passing of civil vehicles during convoy movements. Movement of convoys slow down traffic, they complained. The people, especially the males informed that the hardships thus caused give rise to ill feelings for the Army. They also proclaimed fear for the 'Danda Gadi' at the back of the convoys.

These people liked to ignore the threat of IED blasts and suicidal attacks on convoys should such measures not be adopted by the Army.

The elderly at the gathering informed that the militants use the mountain ridges to filter into Sopore, Baramulla and Handwara in the hinterland and visit the villages this side to get logistic support. These militants do not spend much time in the villages now as opposed to earlier times and pay well for the support provided.

A village elder makes a point

The elderly and the women informed that the villagers too suffer in the hands of the militants who randomly kill on the basis of suspicion of being informers and the surrenderees.

A widow (name withheld) of Devar village informed that her husband (a surrendered militant) was killed by militants in a measure of reprisal. A duo of a family from Lasipora claimed to have lost a few members of their family to militants. The lady, a widow, narrated that her husband late Abdul Majid Dar, who served as a soldier in the Army was first made to put up his papers under duress by the militants and then killed after he had resigned. His decision to quit the Army was influenced by the threats of elimination of the entire family by militants. Majid's widow hopes for and awaits a promised job in the state government.

Intense listening

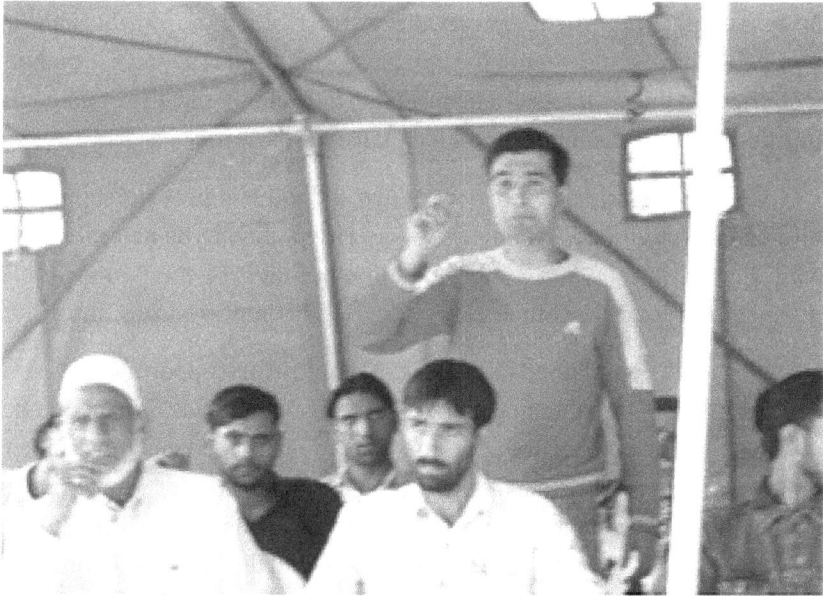

The youth in conversation

Seen with Some of the Locals at Lolab

Though everybody spoke of disillusionment with militancy and grieved the losses of family members yet the warmer blood did not hesitate in saying that they would not mind earning a few thousands acting as conduits or couriers of the militants. The militants they claim, pay better amounts for information and support provided than does the Army.

These people asserted that very few individuals provide support to militants in the villages while a vast majority prefers to be neutral. They claim that taking the side of any one, the militants or the Army, would invoke the wrath of the other.

The youth complained of the lack of employment opportunities in the area specific and the state in general. This they assert causes many to turn towards militancy overtly or covertly. The youth alleged that government jobs are hard to find and in a family where one member holds a government post another too finds a post. They however, displayed keen interest in joining the Army or the Para-military services and desired that recruitment rallies be organised at least at Lolab. They also complained that information about recruitment rallies held elsewhere in the district or nearby district hardly reaches them. Pamphlets and posters at townships are deliberately destroyed by vested interests. They would like a better information system in place.

A lot of displeasure was shown at the political indifferences that is metted out to the people. They alleged that political parties and their leaders approach them only for seeking votes during election. They announced that voting is their constitutional right and they will exercise their right.

They are not averse to the idea of self employment with some financial and infrastructural assistance provided to them but hesitate in turning towards banks for assistance. Bank officials they allege ask for bribes for sanctioning loans. Their livelihood comes basically from seasonal cultivation of paddy, small businesses and for a few in the villages from nefarious activities.

The people alleged that no NGO or Human Rights Organisation has ever reached them or worked with or for them.

Trehgam (North Kashmir)

The people in and around Trehgam are generally educated with approximately 50% of the population having attained graduation level (as per local estimation). It was informed that various governmental schemes for education are functional at schools even in far flung areas.

Employment is an issue here and absorption of the educated is maximum in the education sector. Government jobs they inform are hard to find. The people in the gathering informed that recruitment to SPOs (Special Police Officers) too had not taken place in a year plus time and alleged that in such recruitment drives, preference is always given to ex-militants.

The author seen interacting with locals at Trehgam

The residents categorically pointed out that their political leaders are seen and heard only during elections. Public works are not undertaken and other than the main road in the township no link road is even maintained by the government department concerned. Block development sector, they stated, is non functional.

The people interacted with informed that the Army has been present there since 1947 much to their benefit and that they have faced no problems because of its presence. They admitted that many people get employment by providing ancillary support to the Army. They showed their gratitude to the Army as it has provided them with schools, bus stand sheds, public toilets, tube wells etc. and continues to provide health and medical facilities . These people informed that during the winter months when the upper reaches remain cut off due to snowfall, it is the Army that provides the people living there with ration and other household utility items. They strongly feel that the Army delivers what their state administration should and delivers at a much faster and efficient manner. They admitted that they would rather approach the Army to get public works done.

The gathering comprising men folk said that their women folk feel free and safe to move around in the presence of troops.

Asked if they would like the Army to withdraw, these people answered in the negative, for in its presence, they said, they find security.

The people interacted with in Trehgam said that NGOs and HROs do not reach them.

Another issue brought to light by this gathering was regarding the return of the Kashmiri Pundits. They claimed that the Pundit settlements were till date untouched at least in Trehgam and wanted the Pundits to return to their soil and property.

Balapur (South Kashmir)

The approach to Balapur was made through Awantipora, Pulwama and Shopian towns. At the outer, fringe of Shopiyan town were seen enormous houses which wear a haunted look. These were once occupied by Kashmiri Pundits whose departure from there, it was informed, has affected the education sector.

Frozen in the milieu

The gathering of Balapur consisted of a cross section of people from villages of Shopiyan and Budgam. They did not miss the opportunity to inform about the alleged rape and murder of Asiya Jan and Neelofar Jan. Shopiyan had been burning and in the news over the case. But nobody in the gathering took a stance regarding the case.

Interacting with the people of Shopiyan and Budgam

The district PDP President, Mr Mohammad Shafi Bhat took the lead in speaking on behalf of the people and gradually more and more voices came to the fore.

It emerged that people were generally afraid of the troops prior to 1997-98. They admitted that the troops were harsh on them, often resorting to beatings to extract information on presence and movement of militants. This trend they informed has taken a turn since then. They alleged that the members of the Special Task Force and the Police have inflicted more atrocities on the people. Few of the people present at the gathering had been victims of the militant atrocities, suffering bullet injuries and the like. One of them is on artificial limbs as a consequence to the injuries caused to him by militants.

They remain in constant fear of militants and elimination, should they display much pro-state, peace and development tendencies. Militants, they informed, now-a-days do not spend much time in villages as compared to earlier times. They also informed that only a few in villages provide shelter and other logistic support to the militants, most of the people remain neutral to such activities.

In one to one interaction with people at Balapur

According to the elders present, there must have been at least 30-35 cases of militant brutalities in and around Shopiyan and almost as many in Budgam. These incidences they said have never been reported or highlighted. Most heinous among them are the beheadings. (Refer to Annexure 4 for a glimpse at other atrocities caused on women and children all over Kashmir). The grievance of the people lies in the fact that such cases have never been brought to the fore by any HRO, NGO or the media. NGOs, they alleged , exist only in paper and name and are totally dysfunctional HROs do not reach them – have never reached them.

The Army, they admitted , has contributed much for the development of the area through Operation Sadbhavna. They said that the Army does for them what otherwise should be done by the civil administration. The headman of Pinjora village went on to say that they do understand that innocents getting killed in crossfire does not mean intentional killing.

Various others voiced that if the troops had earlier resorted to slapping and beatings, it was because the people did not cooperate with them and had lied on militant information.

Health centres and dispensaries the people informed, are there sans doctors and medicines. Government doctors hardly reach the centres and if they do, then it is only to mark the attendance register. It is the Army, they said, that provides them with free medicines in far flung areas and caters to their medical needs.

Anantnag (South Kashmir)

Interaction here was with a gathering of 25-30 people comprising mostly of the educated section, women and youth.

The people pointed out that there is essentially a lack of good governance and funds, especially Central funds are not utilised properly. Corruption in the state, they alleged, is rampant and the police they said is not untouched by it.

They opined that injustice has been done to the Kashmiri people by the Centre and their own leaders since Independence. The rigged elections of the past, the people alleged are the root cause of most of the trouble today.

The people were of the opinion that Kashmiris themselves do not help each other and are not united in rightful causes. Now, they said Kashmiris are even indifferent to each other's sufferings. The attitude being 'okay, it is not me or anyone from my family in the line of any militant atrocity so why should I bother ?'[6]

They informed that stone pelting by youngsters and participation in rallies, protests etc is done on payment to them by various organisations. The people here also informed that the fear of reprisal by militants causes many to be mute spectators or indifferent. No one wants to be known as a sympathiser of the militants or the state.

A one to one interaction at Anantnag

---

[6] This appears to be quite a contradiction to the mass protests and stone pelting episodes that are so often witnessed as a united fight for the right of the people of Kashmir.

The gathering informed that the Army provides them security cover and that they place more faith in the Army than the Police. They also informed that the Army did indulge in certain atrocities like beatings (rest not specified) from around 1990 to 94 but that is no longer prevalent.

According to some, demonstrations against the Army happen when people are motivated by vested interests. Even road accidents involving Army vehicles become an issue to be agitated about whereas innumerable accidents involving civil vehicles are just ignored. Motive behind such agitations is just to draw as much monetary benefit from the Army as is possible.

The people acknowledged the Army's contribution in the development of the area and displayed gratitude that it continues to do so.

The women present in the gathering (all three widows) informed that in the villages women folk are in no fear of troops and go about their ordinary chores normally.

The ladies lift the veil

These ladies (all victims of militant atrocities) said that though the State Government had given them the ex-gratia payment, it is the Army that has undertaken to look after their wards' education and their source of sustenance.

Asked if the people would genuinely want the Army to leave, the response was an unanimous negative.

All in the gathering informed that no Human Right Organisation (HRO) or NGO has ever come to work with them or for them, and that the State Human Rights Commission (SHRC) is defunct.

Wuzur (South Kashmir)

At a gathering in Wuzur or Wuzru (as it is also known as) comprising of a cross section of society it evolved that people want peace and a political solution to the Kashmir issue. The people expressed that the cause called Kashmiriyat is long lost and that it is only the vested interests that disturb peace.

Waiting to hear and to be heard

Their society is as much affected by unemployment as by corruption at various levels. The people pointed out the trend that in a family where one member holds a government job, another of the same family finds an appointment too. The people alleged that political party cadres are often rewarded with appointments in Govt. departments. Middlemen, they said, take amounts promising jobs in Govt. departments which many cannot afford to cough out. This money, they alleged, goes to patwaris, ministers and other politicians. Such reasons ultimately prompt the youth to take up arms – not to fight corruption but more to earn the promised amount upon doing so.

The people claimed that they are simply fed up of the politicians who rule the roost and are seen and heard in their midst only before elections. Grants allotted to the people of Kashmir by the Centre, they alleged, does not reach the very people and post elections their MLAs and ministers become total unapproachable.

A local headman speaks for a less fortunate village elder

Taking turns to interact

In so far as the Army is concerned, the people said that troops had committed certain atrocities prior to 2005. They cited a classic case of disappearance of one Mohd Yusuf Wani S/o Gulam Mohd Wani of Dariyan, Daulatabad around the year 1992. Yusuf, they said, was picked up by an Army patrol and was never seen or heard again. Since his disappearance, his father died and his mother became insane.

However, they iterated that ever since 2005 the attitude of the Army towards them has changed and it is a lot friendlier . They said that earlier the people had no trust in the Army but now they accept troops as their brethren. The crowd did not shy away in admitting that there have been innumerable militant atrocities on the people and in that there has been no respite.

The people admitted that they have benefitted from the Army through Operation Sadbhavna with its various schemes and projects. The Army, they said, is looking after the education of many of their wards. This they submitted, would not have been possible had it not been for the Army.

In remote areas, the people said, it is the Army that helps people and not the State Government with its various apparatus.

They alleged that there are Health Centres and dispensaries to cater to the medical needs of the people in and around Wuzru and in the far flung areas, but neither is any doctor to be found there nor any medicines. In such circumstances they either have to go to the major townships or to Srinagar or approach the Army. Mostly, they said , it is the Army that comes to their rescue and supplies them with medicines and medical attention.

The people pointed out that to think Human Rights are violated only by the Army would be a mistake and, that more violations are committed by people in the civil administration and by the militants. These things however, they said, go unnoticed and ignored.

A former militant narrates his woes

Speaking of the feeling of being a part of India amongst them, the elderly present at the gathering said that Amarnath Shrine Board crisis should teach every Kashmiri the lesson that should 'India' decide to just choke NH1A beyond the Banihal Pass, every Kashmiri would starve within no time. And this , they believed, a few have well understood.

The Troops-What They Face / Encounter

In an endeavour to understand what the troops come face to face with in their mission of countering militancy in J&K especially in the Kashmir Valley, interactions at various places in Kashmir were undertaken. These interactions were held right from the unit to the Command Headquarters level of the Army and the Headquarters level of the BSF. What follows is a cumulation of the interactions. For the sake of clarity it has been divided into three parts :–

(a) Interactions with troops of the Rashtriya Rifles (RR).

(b) Interactions with men of the Home and Hearth battalions; and

(c) Interaction at Headquarters Border Security Force (BSF) Kashmir Range.

As mentioned earlier in Chapter IV, the Indian Army had raised the Rashtriya Rifles (RR) as a counter insurgency force. The RR works in coordination with the Police and Para-military forces under the directions of a unified civil-military headquarters.

Maintaining normalcy, assisting in law enforcement by State agencies besides countering terrorism are some of the important functions of the RR. The RR is required to carry out cordon and search, seek and destroy missions. The RR operates bearing in spirit and action an 'Iron fist in a velvet glove' in and around population centres primarily. Special care is taken to avoid subjecting locals to hardships and causing collateral damage during such missions.

Besides the above mentioned activities, a considerable amount of its efforts and resources are utilised in degrading logistic support provided to militants by locals and in weaning them away from militants and militancy.

Troops in the RR are drawn from the regular Army comprising of men from all over the country. Aiding the RR battalions in counter terrorism are also units of the Home and Hearth battalions of the Territorial Army. The raising of the Home and Hearth battalions has gone a long way in meeting the aspirations of the local population. According to Lt Gen (Retd) YM Bammi 'the realization that they will be guarding and protecting their own villages and homes has brought about great enthusiasm in these soldiers'.[1]

(a) **Interactions With Troops of the RR** The troops are sensitised by their leadership on the principles of Human Rights and at all levels care is taken not to violate them. Respecting the culture, tradition and religion are standards to be maintained by the men at all costs. They are indoctrinated to be extremely cautious while carrying out operations and even in mingling with the people. In fact they have orders not to interact at all with civilians on their own. This comes as a result of various sour experiences which the Army has had to face when in 'direct contact' with the civilian population. There have been instances when soldiers have been trapped by civilians to extract monetary benefits either directly from them or indirectly from the Army by slapping charges of Human Rights violation or by threatening to do so.

While combating militants and militancy a soldier, who has been trained to fire effectively to kill, is restrained not only by civil laws but also the 'Commandments' of the COAS. The militants have well understood the restrictions / handicaps that the troops have and take advantage of them.

Unrestricted movement of people at night poses a problem as much a threat especially when ambushes are laid. Often militants use women and OGWs as shields to move from place A to B at night while concealing weapons under their 'ferun'. In such a situation though the troops may be

---

[1] War against Insurgency and Terrorism in Kashmir- Lt Gen YM Bammi.

in complete knowledge of the person being shielded to be a militant, they can neither apprehend nor open fire nor search. In drawing too close, they may be fired at or may jeopardise the lives of people shielding them. This may result in a case of Human Rights Violation (HRV).

As per the laid down procedures, ladies cannot be searched and premises occupied by them cannot be entered into or searched by troops without taking the assistance of lady police personnel. Whereas, on ground, lady police personnel are hard to find in the outskirts of townships and in remote areas. And even if they are, they cannot be expected to be present during the night when ambushes are laid.

Troops are not allowed to enter into any premise unless accompanied by the Police whereas many a times especially at nights, Police personnel are hard to find; more so in remote areas. This as a fact is well known to the militants and they take full advantage of it.

Road Opening Parties (ROPs) are not allowed to open fire, which becomes a practical problem for them when faced by a violent mob. The troops have only to take cover or call for police help which may take precious time to reach. For instance, an Army convoy was stopped in the Srinagar – Baramulla route by protestors, pelted at, mounted and extensively damaged, while all that the troops could do was watch it happen. It was too late by the time help could reach them. There have been instances of burning Army vehicles too. Should troops open fire, be it in the air, it amounts to breaking of Standard Operating Procedure (SOP) or instantly filing of HRV case.

Though the troops are aware that the organization supports them in times of need, yet they feel much more can be done to hold their hands. The Army goes strictly by its laid down set of rules / orders. Not always are the men at fault but the Army takes no chances and initiates enquiries against the individuals named, should any case or alleged HRV be brought up to it. The guilty, if proved, troops admitted must be punished.

Court cases against individuals stretch for years and they have to appear before the local court even after retirement. To do so they may have to travel the length and breadth of the country.

The 'Do's and Don'ts levied on troops put them on the defensive and give every opportunity to the militants and their sympathisers to make the first move and fire first or escape using human shields. Militants are often just allowed to escape out of population centres with the hope of being able to nab them elsewhere in the outskirts.

A peculiar trend of extracting money from the troops / Army in certain parts of the Valley has emerged especially in areas astride the highway (NH1A). The trend is to draw money from passing convoys should an accident happen or is deliberately made to happen by a civil vehicle. Apparently, civil vehicles try to overtake Army vehicles while drawing very close to the latter. Should the vehicle just brush past in the attempt, then the Army vehicles are stopped, 'gheraod' by the locals and presented with a compensation demand. The agitators threaten to slap a case of HRV until the civil driver is paid the amount demanded.[2]

In October 2009 a civilian tempo had overturned on a slippery curve on the Srinagar – Qazigund route much before on Army vehicle was to pass that way. Seeing the Army vehicle approach, people blocked the road and alleged that the tempo was hit by the Army vehicle . They threatened to slap a case of HRV if any compensation was not paid then and there. The helpless driver not wanting a HRV case against him paid an amount of Rs. 2500 and only then was he allowed to pass.

It is always alleged that convoy movements slow down traffic and do not allow any civil vehicles to pass or overtake them and that civilian drivers are afraid of the 'Danda Gadi'. On the contrary, military drivers pray that no civil vehicle draws too close for their comfort or be hit by one lest they have to dole out money or fight to defend themselves in a HRV case.

People often lie about militant presence in their midst to Army patrols, either by choice or under pressure, and do not like troop interaction with certain sections.

---

[2] This phenomenon was also corroborated by civilians in certain places. Ref : Chapter VI. Public Interaction at Anantnag.

It is approximately 10 per cent of the people in an area who are not cooperative with the Army or the state apparatus and draw monetary benefits in lieu of the services provided to militants. The militants now prefer to pay for the logistic support and information provided to them by the people rather than take it by force as done earlier.[3]

Often, people hurl abusive words and language at troops calling them 'dogs' and 'Indian dogs' to say the least. Especially, patrol and ambush parties are at such receiving ends. Sometimes these people also spit at as a mark of disgrace to the troops. Such actions by a section of the population hurt the dignity and self respect of the men in uniform who have to hold back all emotions and any kind of retaliatory action.

Not everywhere in the Valley do troops face such outrageous public behaviour. Public attitude towards troops is dictated by the presence of Jamaatis in the area. The more the numbers of Jamaatis in an area, the lesser is the cooperation with security Forces. These are also areas where one may observe more terror and anti-establishment activities. Elsewhere, ordinary folks cannot seem to be bothered about what happens in major townships or the capital city. They are neither anti-Army nor feel any threat from Army men. In fact, in the Army's presence they find security and do not want the Army to leave.

Militants do not spend much time in villages now, nor do they forcefully enter into houses in villages. Besides Security Forces, they target the Police and suspected informers. There have been incidences when personal scores were settled by the people through militants and militants settled their personal scores too. In 2009 militants shot dead a mother daughter duo at Sopore because the daughter had refused to marry a militant.

To instill fear amongst informers and anybody aspiring to aid Security Forces gruesome killings have taken place. An informer was allegedly beheaded and his head put on display.

The women folk often resort to stone pelting after search operations though nothing untoward may have happened during the conduct of the

---

[3] This was corroborated by locals too. Ref Chapter VI. Public Interaction at Lolab.

same and all rules and regulations abided by. When faced by these hostile ladies, the troops become helpless and on many occasions, may have let militants escape. Otherwise, women are apparently comfortable in the presence of troops and go about their daily normal chores.

People, especially in the villages all over the Valley, approach the Army to get benefits of Operation Sadbhavna and even try to get civil projects done by the Army. According to them the Army delivers and does that faster than any other state agency. But there have been instances where solar lanterns, water pumps and other utility items given by the Army in service to the people, were sold or plundered by the same civilians.

Troops acknowledged the fact that there has been a decline in terror incidences, and the peoples' attitude towards terrorists/militants and militancy is undergoing a change from support to indifference.

(b) **Interaction with troops of the Home and Hearth battalions** The Home and Hearth battalions were raised to meet the aspirations of the people of J&K while reducing unemployment and channelising the misguided youth . These battalions are a curious mixture of ordinary village boys, Ikhwans (ex terrorists) and surrendered militants of various tanzeems including the LeT.

They, like other Territorial Army (TA) battalions, from a vital link between the Army and the people . Their contribution towards the success of Amarnath Yatra post the Amarnath Shrine Board crisis as well as their contribution in the smooth running of the Parliamentary and state Legislative Assembly elections account for some of their operational successes. They have been instrumental in the surrender of militants including that of Sayeed Moinullah Shah (Foreign militant of HM). With multiple other operational successes, they are the proud recipients of various awards as recognition of their achievements.

Coming from the background that they do, service in the Army, they claimed raises their social status. At the same time they fear that members of their families left behind in the villages may become potential targets of militants. They worry that local militants would seek revenge on them as the militants keep themselves abreast with who in the villages serve the

Army or other security agencies.

The Ikhwans, surrenderees and men who have suffered losses at the hands of militants, live under the constant fear of elimination and threats to life from Pak trained militants primarily (foreign terrorists – FTs). This perceived threat is substantiated from diary entries and other recoveries made during operations, besides word of mouth.

They apparently, are identified and marked as priority one targets by active militants either seeking revenge or aiming to deter those who may be considering to join the mainstream.

Hundreds of Ikhwans and members of their families have been killed, tortured and brutalised by militant groups, especially the HM. Beheadings and gruesome display of the heads thereafter, are common methods of terrorising and lesson teaching.

A former Ikhwan informed that he has suffered the loss of three members of his family and that all three were beheaded. Many others of his family were shot at and injured, and his house gutted in 2002-03. Yet another informed that eleven of his family members, both immediate and extended, were killed by members of the JKLF.

The surrenderees are ostracised and members of their family branded as 'traitors' just as they are. They claimed that most of them can not return to their respective villages to settle down there, post retirement.

Presently they are not granted too many days leave at a stretch as it makes them vulnerable and soft targets. A constant system of reporting is in place to check on the safety and well being of these men during their absence from their units. They are accommodated in protected areas during deployment as also when on leave. There is no provision for their disengagement from continuous combat nor is there any provision for their battalion's movement to any peace time locale within the state or outside.

Men of these battalions revealed that local village boys no longer want to go across the border to join militant camps in POK or Pakistan, but are keen on joining Security Forces. Seeing the kind of honour that a martyred soldier receives as Late Sepoy Muzaffar Ahmed Bhatt (recipient of Sena

Medal 2009, of Pulwama district) did, more and more boys want to join the Army.

They pointed out that people who assist the militants, do so out of fear or for money, others prefer to be neutral. They behave in this opportunist manner because they have to remain in the same society and do not want to be branded as traitors to the society.

(c) **Interaction at Headquarters BSF, Kashmir Range** Though the BSF is not deployed in counter insurgency operations currently, it was the first to be deployed in the Valley to combat insurgency there. It had its own share of involvement in operations along the border and CI Ops in the 90s. Going by reports and accounts, this Para-military force is also accused of violations of Rights of the people of J&K. During deployment in the conflict zone of J&K, the Force was treated as aliens but gradually the perception (it was informed) of the people changed. The people began to accept the Force's presence. Contributing to this were the welfare works undertaken by the BSF and the atrocities committed by militants on the people.

It was informed that public perception of Security Forces (SFs) has been very wrong and that there are more numbers of alleged and perceived violations of Human Rights than in reality are. The motives behind such allegations are mainly to draw monetary benefit coming in the form of compensation, personal settling of scores between individuals and the like. Of all the alleged cases of violations of Rights, only a bare minimum have been proved true against the personnel of the Force. The conviction rate is estimated to be 90 per cent. Alleged cases of rape, molestation and misbehavior have been thoroughly investigated and punishment has been awarded to the guilty. It came to light yet again that civilians especially women do indulge to extract monetary benefits.

It was mentioned that till date the people approach the BSF for drawing benefits of welfare schemes on the lines of Operation Sadbhavna of the Army.

The BSF has helped re-build schools, set up medical camps, has organised Bharat Darshan for the children below poverty level in 1997-98. These efforts yielded great results in bringing the people closer to the Forces.

Confirming earlier finding, it came to light yet again that foreign mercenaries / terrorists do not have much influence on the people now as against earlier. Though the people have suffered these atrocities, particularly the women, renegades and suspected informers, they fail to report them for the fear of reprisal. Reprisals come in the form of gang rapes and brutal murders. (Refers to Annexure 4 for details). Fence sitting is done by people as a way to survive. The Police too is not unaffected by the 'need to survive' effect and faces the fear of the unknown.

Despite best efforts made by the SFs, it is observed that when in a crowd, people are always against them. These are times when anti-SFs and ant-India slogans are chanted as a ritual and stone pelting and destruction of public property are resorted to. In the direct line of attack come the SFs who are instructed to act with restraint. To show patience is what is ingrained in them by their leadership.

It was pointed out, that the media often acts against the SFs and does not project the correct picture. It sells what is sold best.

With regard to the book 'Did they vanish in thin air?' by Mr Zahir-ud-din dealing exclusively with enforced disappearances wherein at least twelve cases of the BSF's involvement is recorded, it was opined that not every case may be true. There could be cases of mistaken identity as well since other SFs were also in operation round that time. It was mentioned that if any of the cases were proved true back then, action against the offenders has been taken. Importantly, the BSF will be willing to re-visit cases if there is substantial proof against it.

Interaction with the Men in Uniform

8 For the People of Kashmir- Operation Sadbhavna

With the noble aim of weaning people away from militancy and winning their hearts and minds (WHAM), as also in aid to the civil administration, the Army had launched Operation Sadbhavna in J&K with its multi-faceted projects.

The focus of Operation Sadbhavna is on education, women empowerment, infrastructure development, health and sanitation, conducting motivational tours, sports etc.

In this direction Army Goodwill Schools, equipped with modern educational facilities like computer and science laboratories , sports and transport facilities are being run by the Army and RR formations all over the Valley. A concerted effort by the management of the school is made to employ qualified local teaching staff. The quality of education imparted in these schools coupled with a healthy educational environment in these schools, has made them immensely popular with the locals.

The Army has assisted in the upliftment of existing constructions on infrastructure development at places likes Wallingu, Nar, Pathadialgam etc besides establishing a Army Goodwill School (complete with a Boys Hostel at Boniyar)

North Kashmir / CIF (K) Force

Besides running nine Army Goodwill Schools, the Force /Army has conducted 'Watan ki Sair' or the educational/ motivational tours for children. These tours to as far as Tamil Nadu, Delhi etc have exposed children to the rich social and cultural heritage of our country as well as provided them a glimpse of the pace of development and progress across the country. Interactions with dignitaries during such tours have been a source of inspiration to the participants.

With President

With Chief Minister, Delhi

Governor of Tamil Nadu

Army Goodwill School Budkod

Army Goodwill School Muzbug

Army Goodwill School Margund

Army Goodwill Schools Satbudkot, Mazbugand Margund

Chandigam, a small remote village in Lolab has been transformed into a model village. A Community Development Centre, Primary Health Centre and a shopping complex have been constructed. Besides electrification, beautification and other renovation works, an 800 m track has been constructed therein.

Model Village Chandigam

Shopping Complex

Primary Health Centre

Community Devp Centre

Chandigam

Construction of roads, tracks and bridges under Operation Sadbhavna has not only reduced the hardship of the people but has assisted in improving their socio-economic status. To provide the people with pure drinking water, the Army has undertaken the setting up of tube-wells and hand-pumps in remote places under its area of responsibility. 144 Micro Hydel Projects and 158 solar lights have been installed to benefit approximately 2743 houses in far flung villages.

Inauguration of Bridge

Provision of Hand Pump

Provision of CMPTR for Govt Middle School

Other Projects Under Op Sadbhavna

MICRO Hydel Projects

In order to provide medical aid to remote villages, medical and veterinary camps are regularly organised by units. These camps are organised in close coordination with civil medical authorities. Doctors from the civil and military, together attend to the needy patients and animals. Estimates say around 60,027 locals and 30,000 domestic animals have benefitted from such camps till now.

Medical and Veterinary Camps

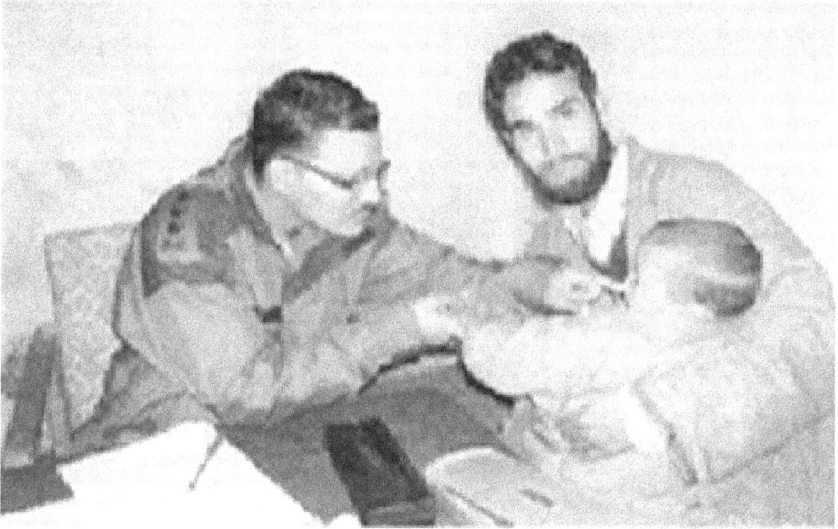

Medical Camps

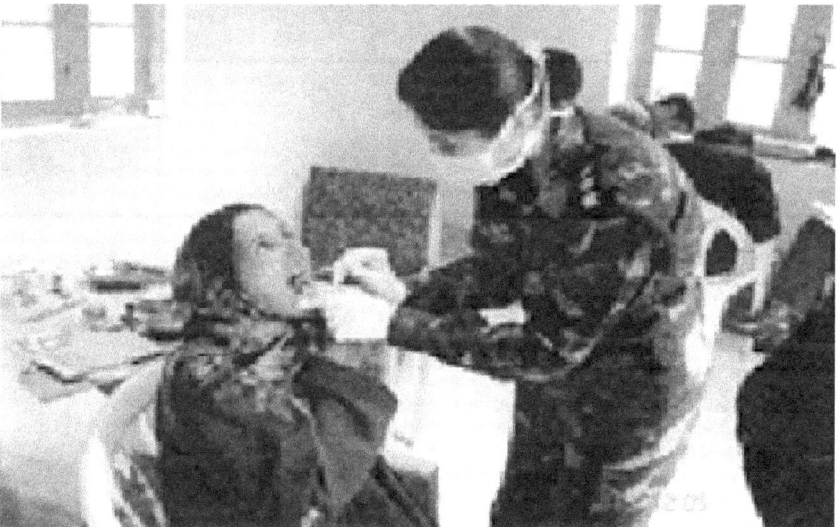

Veterinary Camps

To equip women with basic skills for the management of small scale manufacturing, Vocational Training Centres have been set up under Operation Sadbhavna. These centres impart and enhance skills in knitting, embroidery and computer operation.

Vocational Training Centres

The construction of the Ganderbal and Bandipur multipurpose sports stadia is an effort to channelise the youth in constructive activities and excel in the field of sports. The Force has undertaken to provide sports facilities and kits to schools and villages for constructive engagement of the youth and to divert their mind from militancy.

INAUGURATION OF GANDERBAL SPORTS STADIUM

GANDERBAL SPORTS STADIUM

GANDERBAL SPORTS STADIUM

Sports Facilities Provided Innorth Kashmir

BANDIPUR SPORTS STADIUM

BIRD'S VIEW OF STADIUM

GYMNASIUM EQUIPMENT AT STADIUM

Following the legacy of 'Jawan aur Awam, Aman hai Mukam' (Peace being the ultimate goal for the soldier and the people), various sports events have been periodically arranged by the Army to give the locals an opportunity to showcase their skills and talents.

Organisation of Sports Events

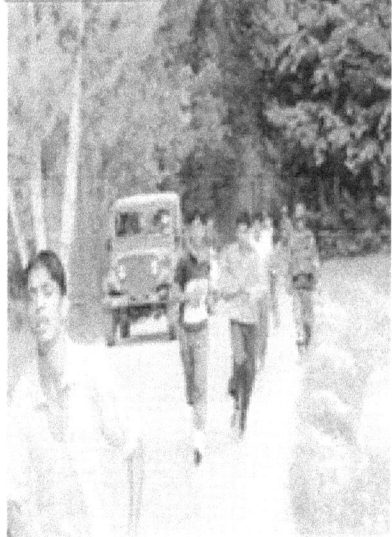

South Kashmir / CIF (V) Force

Besides running Army Goodwill Schools at places like Wuzur, Boniyar, etc the Army has organised local excursions and motivational tours. Students and teachers of Budgam, Shopiyan and Pulwama districts have been on such trips right up to Chennai, Bangalore, Mysore etc.

Army Goodwill Schools at Balapur, Boniyar and Wurur

Projects like electrification schemes, Computer Training Centres, Vocational Training Centres, Community Development Centres, water supply schemes, construction of drainage system, bus stands, waiting sheds, bridges, hostels etc have been successfully completed by the Force.

Electrification, Water Supply Schemes and Vocational Training Centres

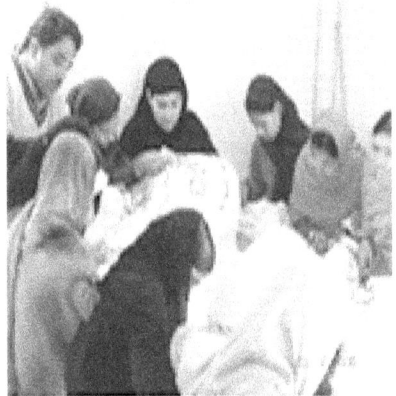

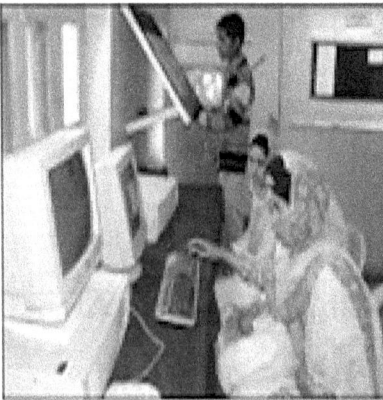

Empowering Women, Construction of Waiting Sheds, Drainage Systemaspart of Opsadbhavna

Places such as Magam, Waltingu Nar, Gaoran, Kuther, Pushru, Shangus, Andhu, Boniyar, Khundru besides others under the area of responsibility of the Army have benefitted immensely from such schemes and projects.

Construction of Bridges

Boys School Complete With a Boys Hostel

As a matter of fact, the township of Waltingu Nar was extensively damaged by avalanches in 2005. The initial rehabilitation was carried out by the Army and thereafter the civil administration had taken over . A primary school building was constructed by the Army after the tragedy.

The Army has constructed 1000 metres of drainage system in and around Khundru.

Afforestation of the park near the office of the Deputy Commissioner, Budgam was undertaken by the Army as part of Operation Sadbhavna. The park is not only utilised by people as a recreational place but also to offer public Namaaz during Muharram. Amenities such as children's park, jogging track, cafeteria, fountains etc were provided by the Army.

Kulgam area is one of the most militancy affected areas and has remained neglected as far as development is concerned. Youth here are driven into militancy. To divert the youth towards some constructive engagements, a sports stadium (the largest so far under Operation Sadbhavna) is being constructed. Besides, there exist a sport stadium each at Shopiyan and Budgam with facilities like track and field, multipurpose gymnasium, cricket pitch, volley ball court, football ground, separate locker and changing rooms for boys and girls with attached toilets. Cafeterias too have been provided with the stadia. Various sports events were organised in such facilities.

The Army has organised medical and veterinary camps in remote villages. There was one such organised in Maspur and Sedhan villages each in Shopiyan district. Public response has been enormous to such camps. Thousands turned up at these medical camps where specailised treatment was provided by civilian medical doctors and lady medical officers of the Army. Facilities for laboratory tests were provided with and medicines were distributed free of cost. Health education regarding family welfare, water borne diseases etc was imparted.

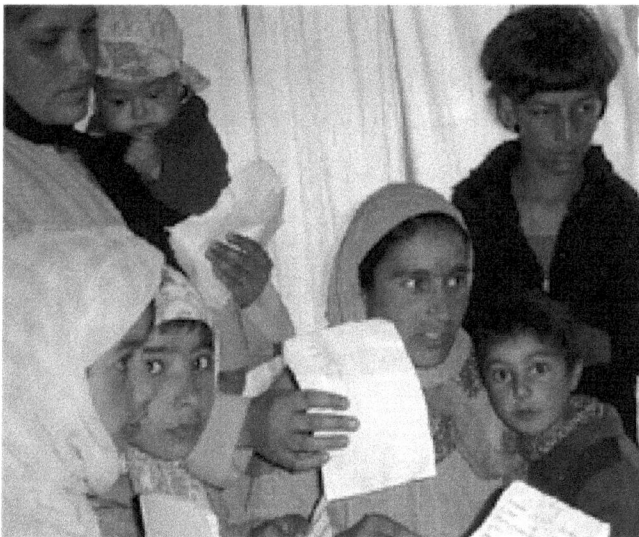

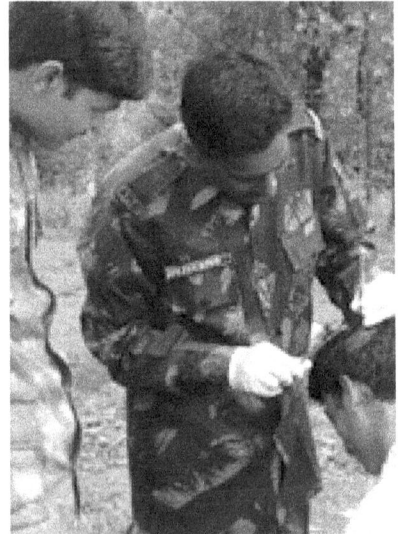

Medical Camps

Similarly at Boniyar, artificial limbs, walking aids and wheel chairs were provided to the needy. This practice was kept up in camps at Lassipora in Pulwama district and in Pucchal (mainly for Gujjars and Bakharwals), as also, in Kulgam and Behibagh. All these camps have not only treated patients requiring medical attention but have also gone a long way in breaking the ice and removing inhibition from the minds of the people about the Army.

Aiding Walk at Various Locations

For the treatment of domestic animals, several veterinary camps have been organised and thousands of animals especially sheep, cattle, poultry, ponies, dogs etc have benefitted.

Veterinary Camps

The Army has undertaken projects on similar lines not only in the Valley but elsewhere in the state too. It has undertaken to sponsor the education of many needy and meritorious children in J&K. In Reasi (Jammu) the Army even runs an orphanage.

In the construction and setting up of most of the projects, locals are engaged which gives them a scope for earning and also the satisfaction of contributing towards the development of their own land.

The success of Operation Sadbhavna lies not only in the effective implementation of the various projects but in that it has brought the people of Kashmir closer to the Army. They realise that the Army works not for the benefit of its ownself but for peace and betterment of the people of Kashmir.

Institutional Roles

In the protection, promotion and upholding of values and principles of Human Rights in J&K the institutional roles of the Indian Judiciary, the National Human Rights Commission and the Army is mention worthy. These institutions stand as democratic assurances to the people that every state apparatus is accountable to them in upholding their rights and freedom. All cases of alleged violation of Rights of the people are tried vide various sections of the law of the land and justice is delivered. As it is for the people elsewhere in the country, it is also for the people of J&K to have faith in the judicial procedures and the judicial system.

Judicial Apparatus

The State

The existence of an independent and impartial judiciary is an essential condition to a federal form of government. The federal judiciary is to act as the custodian of the Constitution, protecting the supremacy of national law, defending the reserved powers of the states and as the guardian of the constitutional system in general. The Constitution of India has therefore made provision for a Supreme Court.

The existence of a highly mature and developed legal system firmly imbedded in rule of law and the approach of judiciary in safeguarding the basic Human Rights and the majesty of law is amply reflected in the decisions of the Supreme Court and the High Courts.

The Supreme Court has an original as well as an appellate jurisdiction. It exercises its appellate jurisdiction both in civil and criminal cases.

The Supreme Court stands at the apex of an integrated judicial hierarchy vested with the power of acting as the highest court of appeal in all cases arising out of Union Laws.

Its main function is to see that laws are fairly administered and no person seeking justice is denied of it by any court in the country. It acts as a unifying force and laws declared by it are binding upon all courts.

The Supreme Court acts as the custodian of the Constitution of India and protection of the rights of the people. Towards this end, the Supreme Court has been authorised to issue various kinds of writs on individuals, associations and even on governments for the enforcement of Fundamental Rights.

The role of the Supreme Court in respect to the protection of the rights of the citizens and in maintenance of the Constitution makes judicial review by the Court necessary. In India, the scope of judicial review is very limited in view of the exhaustive enumeration of powers of the Union and the states by the Constitution, and also in view of the comparatively easy method by which powers of the Union Government may be enlarged especially in times of emergency. The Supreme Court has the power to nullify acts of the Union Parliament on the ground that such laws are contrary to the provisions of the Constitution but has no power to question the fairness or natural justice of Parliamentary legislation.

The framers of the Constitution intended to make the Supreme Court a powerful body designed more to act as a check upon the arbitrariness of the Executive and violation of the Constitution than upon legislative enactments.

There is judicial insistence on following the principles of natural justice and fair play by authorities who make orders that may have an adverse impact on the right of a person.

The independence of the Indian judiciary against any arm twisting by outside forces plays an important role in safeguarding any legally recognised rights. The fairness of the procedures reflected in our laws and recognition of equality of rights of even aliens by virtue of Article 14 as their fundamental rights should generate sufficient confidence in all our legal system.

The role that the judiciary can play in protection of private and other rights will ultimately depend on the perception of those who have to pay it.

The separation of the judiciary from the executive and legislature and its consequent independence is key to its effective functioning and upholding of the rule of law and human rights.

Judicial impartiality is another aspect of judicial independence. Judicial independence requires that the judiciary be able to function effectively without undue interference from political or other agencies. Without this independence, it is impossible for the judiciary to function as it is meant to. Should it not be independent then there is no hope for the rule of law to flourish and instead violence and impunity will be rife.

The Army

Discipline in the Armed Forces requires quick disposal of offences. In order to achieve this aim, justice in the Armed Forces is administered by various tribunals, vested with varying powers depending on the nature and gravity of offences and ranks of the accused persons. These tribunals are called Courts Martial in the Army, Navy and Air Force.

These courts are constituted under respective Acts, i.e Army Act 1950, Navy Act 1957, Air Force Act 1950. These courts are a kind of service tribunals, being part of the administration of the respective Armed Forces. They are not part of the judiciary. These tribunals are not subject to the superintendence by the High Courts .However, trial by such courts shall be deemed to be a judicial proceeding within the meaning of sections 198 and 228 of the IPC and such court shall be deemed to be a court within the meaning of Section 345 and 346 of the CrPC 1973.

Vide Army Act (1950) Section (1) (vii) 'Court Martial' means a court martial held under the Army Act. 'Court Martial' signifies a court relating to war, military, as distinguished from civil court. This separated category of court has arisen due to certain extraordinary exigencies of the military, particularly in times of war. Supreme importance of discipline in the military makes it essential that matters connected with persons working in it should not normally be left for decision of ordinary court.

As regards the trial of offences committed by Army men, the Army Act draws a three fold scheme. Certain offences enumerated in the Army Act are exclusively triable by a court martial; certain other offences are triable by the ordinary criminal court and certain offences are triable both by the ordinary criminal court and the court martial.

In respect of the last category both the courts have concurrent jurisdiction.

Offences like mutiny, desertion, absence without leave, unbecoming conduct, violation of good order and discipline etc are offences triable exclusively by courts martial.

Murder of a civilian, culpable homicide of a civilian, rape of a civilian while not on active service, out of India or on a frontier post are some of the offences triable by criminal courts only. Offences that are triable by the courts martial as well as ordinary criminal courts are for example counterfeiting coin, public nuisance, causing hurt, wrongful restraint, defamation, insult , kidnapping, abduction etc.

Offences covered by Section 69 of the Army Act and described as civil offences fall in the concurrent jurisdiction of courts martial and ordinary criminal courts and pertain to the third category.

Army Act (1950) Section 69 reads as under :-

Civil offences – subject to the provisions of Section 70, any person subject to this Act who at any place in or beyond India commits any civil offence shall be deemed to be guilty of an offence against this Act, and if charged therewith under this section shall be liable to be tried by a court martial and, on conviction, be punishable as follows, that is to say :-

(a) If the offence is one which would be punishable under any law in force in India with death or with imprisonment for life, he shall be liable to suffer any punishment, other than whipping, assigned for the offence, by the aforesaid law and such less punishment as in the Act mentioned;

(b) In any other case, he shall be liable to suffer any punishment, other than whipping, assigned for the offence by the law in force in India or imprisonment for a term which may extend to seven years, or such less punishment as in this Act mentioned;

Section 70 of the Army Act reads as under :-

'Civil offences not triable by court martial – A person subject to this Act who commits an offence of murder against a person not subject to military, naval or air force law, or of culpable homicide not amounting to murder against such a person or of rape in relation to such a person, shall not be deemed to be guilty of an offence against this Act and shall not be tried by a court martial unless he commits any of the said offences :-

(a) While on active service or

(b) At any place outside India or

(c) At a frontier post specified by the Central Government by notification in this behalf'.

Of the various other offences the following offences which may relate to human rights violations triable at courts martial and punishable under Army Act are :-

(a) Violation of good order and discipline – Any person subject to this Act who is guilty of any act or omission which though not specified in this Act, is prejudicial to good order and military discipline shall on conviction by Court Martial, be liable to suffer imprisonment for a term which may extend to'even years or such less punishment as in this Act mentioned (ref : Army Act, 1950).

(b) Unbecoming conduct – Army officer, JCO or WO who behaves in a manner unbecoming his position and the character expected of him shall, on conviction by court martial, if he is an officer, be liable to be cashiered or to suffer such less punishment as in this Act mentioned; and, if he is a junior commissioned officer or a warrant officer, be liable to be dismissed or to suffer such less punishment as is in this Act mentioned'.

Most of the cases of violation of Human Rights in J&K fall under the above mentioned categories and the offenders have been tried and convicted under courts martial.

The National Human Rights Commission

Realising the need for an independent body for promotion and protection of human rights, the Government of India established the National Human Rights Commission (NHRC). The establishment of an autonomous Commission by the Government reflects its commitment for effective implementation of human rights provision under national and international instruments.

The Commission came into effect on 12 October 1993, by virtue of the Protection of Human Rights Act 1993. (Refer to Annexure 3 for relevant details) The Act contains broad provisions related with its function and powers, composition and other related aspects.

As mentioned earlier[1] the Indian Constitution provides certain fundamental rights for individuals in Part III known as Fundamental Rights. The rights guaranteed in the Constitution are required to be in conformity with the International Covenant on Civil and Political Rights and International covenant on Economic, Social and Cultural Rights.

The responsibility for the enforcement of the Fundamental Rights lies with the Supreme Court by virtue of Article 32 and by Article 226 with the High Courts.

Wide powers and functions have been vested on the NHRC under Section 12 of the Protection of Human Rights Act. Paragraph (a) of Section 12 provides, that the commission can enquire and initiate suo motu action against any public servant against whom a complaint has been registered for violation of human rights. Section 12 (6) provides that that the Commission can intervene in any proceeding involving any allegation of a violation of human rights pending before a Court with the approval of such court.

Section 12 (c) empowers the Commission to visit any jail or other institution with prior intimation to the state government for the purpose of mainly monitoring prison or custodial jurisprudence.

The Commission can make recommendations to state governments on the basis of such visits.

---

[1] See Chapter V. EXISTING RIGHTS, LAWS AND PARADIGM.

Section 12 (d) empowers the Commission to review the safeguards provided under the constitution or any law for the time being in force for the protection of human rights and also to recommend measures for their effective implementation.

Under Section 12 (e) there is a separate provision to review the causes of terrorism, which inhibits the enjoyment of human rights and to recommend appropriate remedial measures.

The Protection of Human Rights Act (1993) outlines the investigative role of the Commission

Public awareness on the work of the Commission can be gauged by the number of cases received by it over the years.

The Commission broadly divides the cases in these following categories

:

(i) Custodial deaths.

(ii) Police excesses (Torture, Illegal detention / unlawful arrest, false implications etc.)

(i) Fake encounters.

(ii) Cases related to women and children.

(iii) Atrocities on Dalits/members of minority community/disabled.

(iv) Bonded labours.

(v) Armed Forces / Para-military forces and

(vi) Other important cases.

In some of the cases, the Commission may opt for a personal hearing with the petitioner or any other person on behalf of the petitioner for appropriate disposal of the matter. This personal hearing will provide an opportunity for examining witnesses, if any, in support of the complaint and hearing evidence in support of the petitioner's stand. Once the commission or any other person under its authority undertakes an investigation, the report of the investigation should be submitted within a week of its completion. In some cases however, the Commission may allow further time for the submission of reports.

Under Section 8 (12), the Commission or any of its members when requested by the chairperson may undertake visits for on-the-spot study and where such a study is undertaken by one or more members, a report thereon shall be furnished to the Commission as early as possible.

Section 19 of the Protection of Human Rights Act (1993) restricts the power of NHRC to initiate investigation on its own in the case of violation of human rights by Armed Forces.

Cases Received by the NHRC and Forwarded to the Army for Investigation

Year	NHRC Cases
1994	17
1995	24
1996	43
1997	139
1998	47
1999	69
2000	151
2001	100
2002	166
2003	32
2004	35
2005	35
2006	29
2007	32
2008	28
2009	45
2010	30

Figure 9.1

Jurisdiction of the NHRC to deal with the complaints against Armed Forces is subject only to restrictive procedure.

It appears from the above provisions that the Commission is a powerful institution but in practice the Commission is powerless when a state government refuses to comply with its recommendation. The Commission is endowed with only recommendatory power and its recommendations are not legally binding.

Assessing the Human Rights Violation Meter in J&K- A Few Case Studies

The deployment of the Army to combat terrorism and such a prolonged exposure to combat has brought it under the ever watchful eyes of various national and international vanguards of Human Rights for violations and alleged violations of Human Rights.

The role played by the media (the press, especially the vernacular press and the electronic media) in such low intensity conflict situation has been either to assuage or to aggravate the sentiments of the local population with their impartial or biased reporting . More often than not, in J&K it has been observed that the media has deviated from the balancing role that it can actually play. There have been numerous incidents of false reporting with the Army being blamed for various excesses as heinous as rape and even murder. Most of these cases on later investigation proved false and motivated.

Reports of alleged killings, fake encounters, custodial deaths and disappearances, rapes and molestation by the SF (especially the Army deployed in J&K), are a regular phenomenon. If these reports are to be totally believed then it would appear that the Army functions sans any accountability, sans may laid down rule or procedure.

What is overlooked in the enthusiasm of guarding the Human Rights of the people by the HROs and the Civil Society in Kashmir, is the fact that any action that may be classified as a crime or a violation of any Right by the Army can be held accountable and subjected to intra-Army judicial procedure. In such procedures verdicts are open to appeal at the level of the

High Courts and Supreme Court. The Army does not function sans any limits on its own personnel. *There is a sound system of inbuilt accountability.* All allegations of Human Rights violations are investigated in detail by appropriate authorities in the Army. Appropriate action is initiated against offenders after a thorough scrutiny of reports and then forwarded to the NHRC, the Ministry of Home Affairs etc through the Ministry of Defence.

The Human Rights cell at the Army Headquarters under the Adjutant General's Branch acts as a nodal agency for receiving allegations from various agencies including the NHRC. It investigates the veracity of such allegations and ensures that corrective action is taken to minimise and prevent Human Rights abuse by the Army. The Army has established Human Rights Cell where deemed necessary, at the Command Headquarters, Corps Headquarters and Divisional Headquarters level to meet the requirements mentioned above. They report to the Army Headquarters Human Rights Cell regarding the same, through the chain of command.

In J&K, every RR Force Headquarters too has a Human Rights Cell which reports up the chain of command to the Army Headquarters.

The Army HQ claims to have received 1450 cases of Human Rights Violation and alleged violation from 1994 to Dec 2010 from J&K and the North East. Therein 1404 cases the HQ claims to have investigated of which 1350 (96%) cases have been proved to be false and baseless and 54(4%) cases have been proved to be true. The Army has punished 129 of its personnel including 38 officers, 12 JCO and 79 other ranks for offences related to Human Rights violations in J&K and the North East.

According to figures available at the Army HQ, the highest number of cases of alleged violations received and forwarded to the Army for investigations by NHRC and Non-NHRC were in the year 2000 (205), followed by 1997 (198) and 2002 (176) respectively.[1] The figures correspond

---

[1] Data as provided by the Human Rights Cell, Army HQ - Sujata Kanungo

with the highest number of terrorists killed in the same years as mentioned above. (Refer to Annexure 1 for details)

From the data available with the author on the nature of cases of Human Rights violations in J&K till March 2007, it can be said that most of the cases are related to the fairer sex (totaling 36) followed by killings (totaling 10), failure to exercise control over subordinates and that of harassment (totaling 9 each).

A few cases studied in 2007 have been listed below to give a glimpse on their nature and extent.

CASE 1.   Excerpts from Case No. NC/HRC/AGN/HRC/11-2008.

The Hindustan Times reported "Molestation sparks protest in Shopyian, 4 hurt," June 2003. Complaint based on the same was given to the NHRC by Shri CB Vinod, National Centre for Advocacy Studies, New Delhi.

The complaint pertaining to the alleged molestation and harassment of some girl students of Shopiyan Girls Higher Secondary and Government College, Shopiyan was investigated and it revealed the following :

On 09 June 2005, troops of 1 Rashtriya Rifles were carrying out routine checking a civil vehicles at Chaudhary Gund for any concealed illegal arms and ammunitions. At 0930 hrs, a civil bus was stopped for checking and all passengers including ladies were requested to debus . Some college girls in the bus resisted the search. However, the SF personnel ensured that the passengers debus in order to enable a proper and systematic check. This was resented by the college girls. The Army officer present on the spot assuaged their feelings. The matter was thus resolved amicably then and there. After the check the bus was allowed to move towards Shopiyan.

However, finding it to be an exploitable opportunity, some anti-national elements managed to play on the sentiments of the local populace by spreading false rumours about molestation of young girls by Army personnel and organised a protest. Significantly, the very girls who were being touted by these anti-national elements, as victims of molestation by Army personnel, came forward and gave a clean chit to the Army personnel in writing, braving all odds. No girl student was ever dragged inside the camp nor was any of them beaten up by the jawans, as was reported in the newspaper.

CASE 2. Case No.C/6227/AG/NC/NHRC/HRC/05-2004

(i) Complaint from Mrs Safina Begum w/o Shri Mohammad Sadeeq. Consider excerpts from the original complaint.

"On 1ˢᵗ October 2003 my husband left his house at about 5 am in order to go to Jammu for giving some money to his elder brother for raising some construction of the house in Jammu.

Thereafter the applicant came to know that on the same day when the late husband proceed from Dharana to Mendhar to catch the bus for Jammu he was picked up by the Army and was taken to some unknown place. On intervening night i.e. 3/4

October 2003 my husband was killed deliberately, intentionally and knowingly for their vested interest by 25 Punjab Regiment. That dated 04-01-2003 the Army authorities handed over the dead body of my husband to the civilian for the purpose of burial in village Lanjote, Tehsil Mendhar, District Poonch,J&K State".

"that the Army has also buried the dead body of my husband as unclaimed body".

"The husband of the applicant who was a school teacher was not at all involved in any militancy related act, nor there such record which can show or prove the involvement of my husband in any militancy related activity".

"The Army personnel with the connivance of some locals has called the husband of the applicant who was quite innocent and was not involved in any militancy related activity and from the persons concerned the applicant has come to know that at the behest of (1) Commanding Officer 25 Punjab Regiment, Post No.481 Sector Mendhar, (2) Daljit Singh 2ⁿᵈ IC, 25 Punjab Regiment, Post No 481, Sector Mendhar, (3) Major Kamal Kashore of 25 Punjab Regiment, Post No.483, Sector Mendhar, with conivance and conspiracy of (4) Mohamad Ayub …………with the criminal intention brutally killed the husband of the applicant and in order to suppress the crime secretly buried the body of late Shri Mohammad Sadeeq in Lanjote dubbing that the killed person was a foreigner who's identity cannot be established ....''

"......................State Government may kindly be directed to pay the compensation amounting to Rs.50,00,000.00 (Rs Fifty lacs only) to the applicant for the killing of her husband and for assistance and education of three young children who are school going because of the fact that the applicant has no source of income as she is only a housewife.

It is further submitted that my eldest son namely Khwaja Ghulam Mustafa 18 years of age may kindly be provided employment in any Government Department on compassionate ground".

(ii) The NHRC had taken cognisance of the complaint

Investigation revealed that based on reliable information about movement of terrorists, an ambush was laid by 25 Punjab in Lanjote. At about 2140 hours on 03 Oct 2003 the ambush party noticed a group of militants trying to infiltrate into Indian territory. On being challenged by the ambush party the terrorists opened fire. The troops retaliated in self defense and in the ensuing fire-fight four terrorists were killed. Two Army personnel also sustained severe injuries during the encounter.

Arms and ammunitions as well as cash was recovered from the site. The dead bodies were handed over to the Police post and an FIR was lodged. None of the dead bodies could be identified at that time by the officials of police post Balakot and the villagers. The bodies were then handed over to the villagers for burial.

Investigations have further revealed that Late Shri Mohd Sadeeq indulged in terrorist related activities and he was not picked up by any personnel of 25 Punjab on 01 Oct 2003 as alleged by the complainant.

The case was also investigated independently by the police authorities.

The OWP 15/2004 has subsequently been withdrawn by the petitioner and the Hon'ble court vide orders dated 13 May 2005, have disposed off the petition.

CASE 3.   Case No.NC/NHRC/HRC/09-2005

Place of incident : Village Thiun , Thesil Kangan, District Srinagar, Jammu and Kashmir.

(i) Complaint from Chiragh for Human Rights, Brooklyn, New York, alleging that on March 12, 2005, troops from 24 Rashtriya Rifles had thrown a cordon around the village Thiun at dawn during which all the men in the village lined up outside while women in their homes were stripped and molested. The complaint alleged that on hearing the cries of the women, the men attempted to rush to their help but were beaten by the troops, leading to many serious injuries. Some of the women escaped further abuse only by jumping out of the first floor windows, in one case holding a three year child. Old women and children too were beaten by the troops .

Further it was alleged that this crackdown was only the latest of 10 (ten) that the village had faced since December 2004, forcing many villagers to migrate, leaving behind their property and means of livelihood.

(ii) NHRC had taken cognisance of the above mentioned case.

Detailed investigation revealed that a cordon and search operation was planned to be carried out by 24 Rashtriya Rifles at village Thiun on 12 March 2005 based on specific intelligence input about movement of terrorists from village Hayan Palpura to Thiun.

Information about the conduct of the operation was given to Police Station Kangan. On 12 March 2005 the cordon was established and an announcement for the search to commence was made by the Moulvi from the village Masjid.

When the search party approached the village, some women and notorious young men attempted to break the cordon. They were warned and physically blocked to obviate any untoward incidents. Some miscreants took advantage of the commotion and spread a rumour about the killing of four villagers by the SF which agitated the crowd. While the gathering was being controlled and dispersed, some villagers started pelting stones at the buses on the National Highway and commenced shouting against the SF.

Intervention by senior Army and Police officials led to dispersal of the crowd. However, in the melee created by some miscreants, few villagers had sustained minor superficial injuries which were not attributable to action by the SFs.

The written statements given by Shri Ghulam Hassan Nazar and Smt Mukul Bano of village Thiun bear testimony to the fact that injury sustained by the civilians was not attributable to any action by the Army personnel, and the women were afforded humane and dignified treatment during the operation on 12th March 2005 in village Thiun. The Sarpanches and Nambardars of the villages in Tehsil Kangan including village Thiun had explicitly certified that the allegations were void of any truth.

The case registered at Police Station Kangan on 12th March 2005 to investigate the incident had been closed as 'Non Admitted'. Investigation report by SSP Ganderbal on the article published in the Kashmir Times, confirmed mischievous intent of the reporter and lack of substance in the allegations of rape/molestation/harassment. It also corroborates the facts given in the detailed report.

Actions Initiated by the Army

On the other hand, the Army personnel who have in fact abberated from the strict rule of operation in insurgency situations have been awarded strict punishment as well. For example :

CASE 1. - Taking suo moto cognisance of a news item published in the Indian Express on 13th June 1998, and after thorough investigations, the Army convicted two Gunners of 313 Field Regiment for committing rape of a woman. They were awarded 10 (ten) years of rigorous imprisonment and dismissed from service on 07 July 1998.

CASE 2. - In a case involving 33 Rashtriya Rifles on 12th August 2006, the Army provided Rs 2,00,000 (Two lakh) each as compensation for the families of Ghulam Moiddin Tantray and Ruby Jann of village Chailpatti (J&K) and house hold goods for the marriage of the daughter of the deceased. The state government too provided Rs.1,00,000 (one lakh) each for the two families and Rs. 50,000 (fifty thousand) for the wedding of the daughter of the deceased. The officer involved was awarded reproof.

CASE 3. - In yet another case, Case No. NHRC/EC/26/99 compensation of Rs.3,00,000 (three lakh) was paid under the sanctioning authority of the Army to the next of kin (NOK) of an actual victim of violation.

Not to forget, Maj Rehman Hussain was cashiered and dismissed from service. In an unprecedented move an officer was handed over to the police by the Army in 2010, in an alleged case of false encounter killing in Rafiabad (Machil Sector) J&K. In the latter case of 2010, the command from the Commanding Officer was removed, as also the accused officer handed over to the police for law to take its own course. The matter is at present sub-judice.

Table 1 of Annexure 5 shows an overall account of cases received by the Human Rights Cell (Army Headquarters) from sources categorized as NHRC and Non- NHRC, covering years 1994 to 2010. It accounts for both J&K and the North East. Vide the table it is observed that the maximum number of cases of alleged violations were received by the Army in the year 2000 (205) followed by the years 1997 (198) and 2002 (176). From the year 2003 the number of cases received by the Army shows a decreasing trend. In so far as J&K is concerned the table reveals a significant drop in the number of cases received by the Army from the year 2003 to 2010, the highest within the said period being 34 (2005) and the lowest being 13 (2004). (For other details pertaining to Human Rights case records refer to Annexure 5)

From the above it can be seen that while a few aberrations have occurred, the Army has been performing its role in CI and CT Operations with commendable restraint. Troops realise the importance of exemplary behaviour and conduct during the sensitive cordon and search operations, especially those involving civilian ladies and children.

The authorities have also been very sensitive to any fault committed by the SFs. Prompt investigations have been initiated and whosoever was found guilty has been severely punished.

The above strategy has enabled the Army to win the confidence of the people in the Valley to quite an exent, though still a section of the population at times opposes the Army – often due to fear of the militants.

11 Towards Resolution

In evaluating the Human Rights record of the Army operating in the Valley one must always take into account the extra-ordinary circumstances and the hostile and opportunist section of population it comes face to face with. People who in a 'protected environment' behave in a manner and when out in mobs and crowds behave in a completely different manner. Winning the hearts and minds of such people can never be an easy task and if the Army is to do it alone then it can never be done. This uphill task has to be undertaken by the political leadership at the Centre and the State, taking the people into confidence. This process must include the moderate faction of the Hurriyat and the youth.

The Centre and the State's Role

The Government and its agencies can take the following few steps towards resolving certain burning issues of Kashmir :

(i)   A political consensus has to be brought about involving all political parties including the moderate Hurriyat in resolving the Kashmir issue. There cannot be any shying away from the Treaty of Accession or the dilution of Article 370.

(ii) The State Government has to do more to reach out to the people which can better be done if elected representatives of the people spend more time in their constituencies. Local MLAs may be asked to visit their respective constituencies at least twice a month if the Assembly is not in session. This can be monitored by the state through the Deputy Commissioners (DCs).

(iii) DCs and SSPs may take turns to regularly visit the tehsils and hold meetings with the village headmen and other responsible elders of villages.

(iv) A system of accountability of state government employees needs to be streamlined to check on prevalent corruption and mal-practices. Appointment of a Lokayukta will go a long way in this direction.

(v) The role of women in combating or sustaining insurgency / militancy in J&K has been immense. Whereas on one hand they have been the worst sufferers, on the other, they have also abetted militancy. They have been successfully used as a first line of defense by militants and have also been brutally raped, tortured and killed by them. Many continue to suffer silently accepting atrocities as their fate until one day one Ruksana arises. Many were killed on mere suspicion of being informers or having refused to marry militants or in trying to wean away their brothers, beaus and husbands away from militancy.

The role of women in the state police force is insignificant as also in CI and CT Operations. Bearing in mind their paramount importance in search and frisk operations especially of women and the handicap faced by troops/ SFs during certain operations, it is suggested that the strength of women be increased in the state police force. Their role in intelligence gathering, weaning and influencing the misguided should not be underestimated but be tapped to the fullest.

Action in this regard will not only generate employment but also true empowerment and inspiration.

(a) The Army has assisted the state government in imparting vocational training courses to scores of women. It is not necessarily true that each of the trained has been able to utilize the acquired knowledge / skill in a gainful manner. It is recommended that those women certified with a skill based knowledge be engaged by the state government in gainful employment opportunities be it in the self employment or the medium or the small scale cottage industry sector. Forming co-operative societies at the village level will go a long way towards the direction.

(b) The youth must be engaged in a meaningful dialogue process.

(c) More skill based employment generation schemes should be developed by the State and Central Governments.

(d)   Apart from keeping diplomatic channels open, the government should also employ a strategy of precision attacks on terror training camps located in POK with minimum chances of collateral damage.

The Army's Role

In so far as the Army and other Security Forces are concerned the following merit immediate consideration :

(i) A proactive stance in Human Rights and media management needs to be adopted.

(ii) A channel of dialogue with leading Human Rights groups and civil society or interactions between the two parties, Army and HROs in the Valley needs to be opened if transparency is advocated.

(iii) The emphasis on Human Rights training and enhancement of men tal and physical robustness of all ranks at the pre-induction level has proved successful. However, as still a few cases of breech of laid down drills and procedure occur, the feasibility of introducing periodic refreshers training through case studies may be examined.

During these refresher capsules, emphasis on human behaviour through specially designed psychological exercises designed and developed by DRDO could also be conducted.   It is felt that these measures will further enhance positive attitude of Commanders at all levels deployed in high stress CI operations and enable them to achieve better results.

(iv) A few instances of alleged fake encounters apparently by a few individuals who may have felt that these may enhance their chances of promotion have been reported in the vernacular or national media. A few Commanders have also been reported to have violated the laid down aim of achieving the national goal of 'bringing peace and normalcy as soon as possible in J&K'.

While the Army has a zero tolerance policy for such cases and these are dealt with severely by the Army authorities, it is suggested that special efforts be made to educate all ranks especially the Commanders at all levels that 'body counts and weapons recovered' are not only the criteria or measures of their successful conduct of CI operations.

(v) In this regard, it is recommended that while gallantry awards for bravery in the face of militant's attacks/encounters, and for out standing devotion to duty should continue to be awarded as at present, the impact created by a unit and sub-unit on the peo ple of its area of responsibility be also considered as an impor tant indicator. In this, the positive results of Operational Sadhbhavna could also be viewed. By adopting this approach even the locals will feel that their 'voice of appreciation' of good conduct of a unit in their area has some value. They are likely to be more forthcoming in supporting the cause of the forces.

(vi) The efforts made by a unit in ensuring human rights of the locals in their area of responsibility and during search and cordon operation and results achieved, should be given heavy weightage while awarding Unit Citation and other awards.

(v) Commanders ought to be careful about how much pressure is to be put on 'result' oriented performance. For more the pressure on the Field Commanders, more are the chances of them making mistakes. Being under pressure they are likely to violate laid down norms and Human Rights to achieve and show better results.

(vi) Commanders should give a more humane touch to the process of sensitisation of troops and make them feel that they too have equal Constitutional and Human Rights.

(vii) For the above mentioned purpose specialists from outside the Army may be roped in to give lectures, talks, etc. Troops must be made to feel that they are cared for by people outside the Army circles too.

(viii) Army may consider appointment of an Ombudsman with particu lar area of operation in J&K and the NE so far as Human Rights issues are concerned. The said Ombudsman should have legal authority over the handling of Human Rights matters and not just be a recommendatory entity.

The Ombudsman can act in consonance with the Courts Martial and the civil judicial apparatus as an independent and third party inclusion into the investigating and reporting procedures.

(ix) Army families could be permitted to visit / reside in safe areas so that the soldiers see the humane face of life. Their children could also study in the local schools especially Army Goodwill Schools. This would enable interaction between children and developing bonds of friendship between the Kashmiris and the so called 'out siders'.

(x) There should be interaction between the Army and the local population in social and cultural activities. The prevailing trend of socia lising on religious festivals is commendable.

(xi) Caution needs to be exercised on 'Danda' drill and whistles giving priority to Army vehicles over civil vehicles. Though such a practice is not much prevalent now.

(xii) As a measure of transparency, trials of Human Rights violation cases could be opened to civilians. Besides showing that cases are tried, this will develop the much desired trust in the fairness of the Army and its functioning in J&K.

(xiii) Following the spirit of the same transparency, the Army from time to time should make it a point to present to the civilian world especially in J&K and the rest of the country the exact facts and figures pertaining to Human Rights violations.

(xiv) Since the situation in J&K and the North East is dynamic, the number of cases of Human Rights violations could be changing every day and every week. Hence it is suggested that the overall figures be updated by the Army Headquarters on a half yearly ba sis and in consonance with both the Northern and the Eastern Com mands.

(xv) The Army can undertake the exchange of students from dependen ts of Ikhwans/renegades with Army Schools outside J&K.

(xvi) The Army is known to have adopted wards of many killed by militants. The orphanage at Reasi is a model example. It can also adopt the wards of killed Ikhwans / renegades and rehabilitae their families. More such institutions should be established with the as sistance of the State Govt.

(xvii) Areas where besides the Army, other Central SFs are operating, a distinction in the combat uniform may be introduced to avoid any kind of confusion over the identity of the troops conducting search operations in population centers.

(xviii) Considering the physical and psychological stress that troops undergo during CI Operations, training in Yoga and meditation could well be incorporated and imparted at the pre-induction level.This will not only help in stress management of the individual soldiers but also enable them to deal with hostility in a more effective, humane and objective manner.

(xix) Other SFs too can carry out goodwill gestures on the line of Op eration Sadbhavna in the Valley. The Border Security Force did carry out such operations when it was deployed in population centers and received favourable response from the people. The Force can continue to do so in the areas that it is deployed now.

The Role of the Media

The role of the media in modern society especially in conflict zones is overarching. It can be an important instrument in the protection of Human Rights by bringing to the notice of the government and the public, cases of Human Rights violations. But in doing so it must be careful about the way it reports the matter. The following guidelines need to be followed:-

(i) The manner in which it reports must not have any adverse effect on societal harmony. Its reporting must be objective.

(ii) The media must take caution that by virtue of its reporting one act of violence does not lead to another act of violence.

(iii) Reporting must be done in such a manner that it does not allow the public to form an opinion or prejudice against any person or institution. One or two ill reputed person should not be allowed to bring the same reputation to the whole institution.

(iv) The media should bring to the fore successes as it should the failure or misdeeds of the government and its organs.

(v) While reporting any matter pertaining to Human Rights violations, a responsible media must bear in mind that the subject of its criticism is presumed innocent till proved guilty in a court of law. The media should not label anybody like a convict unless the accusation against him is proved.

(vi) Decisive reporting must at all costs be avoided as it may have far reaching consequences. Such reporting may leave a totally lopsided impression on the minds of the people. Trial by medial through investigative journalism is a risky exercise and should be avoided.

(vii) The media should cover court proceedings and ensure through its reporting and coverage that the rights of the accused persons are protected and all legal remedies to which they are entitled to are provided to them.

(viii) The media must not allow itself to be used as a tool by vested interests in furthering their cause.

The above mentioned guidelines enumerated for various agencies, if followed with earnest will go in a long way not only in soothing the sufferings of the people of Kashmir but will also restore their faith in the political system of the country. The Kashmiris will have a better understanding and acceptance of the Armed Forces which is there to provide them safety and security and the basic Human Right – the right to life.

Conclusion

The subject of Human Rights violations in the context of counter insurgency operation J&K has been discussed the world over in various forums over the years.

Various human rights groups within the state and outside have been active in bringing to light many incidents and issues before the world audience. Due to increased awareness and instant media accessibility and communication revolution, these incidents have got and continue to get wide publicity. It would not be wrong to say that often such publicity is helpful to the cause of militant organisations and affects the country's image adversely. These incidents tarnish the image of Security Forces engaged in countering militancy and terrorism and alienate them from the masses.

Human Rights violation in the context of low intensity conflict is a highly complex and sensitive issue having moral, legal, political and social implications.

As narrated earlier, in many cases of alleged violations, relatives of militants killed by Security Forces have raised claim of the killed militants being innocent. Articles to that effect have been published in local newspapers to create resentment against the Army and with a view to lowering the morale and tempo of operations. These allegations are labeled at the instigation of the militant organisations to gain mileage and as a propaganda machinery in the hands of the militant organisations, not to forget the financial benefits that can be accrued from the state government and the Army per se.

It has been observed that nobody raises an eyebrow when innocent lives are lost, women are raped and brutally killed by militants, or a child is killed by protestors and demonstrators. Destruction of properties by stone peltors, disruption of normal life because of unending agitational politics and protests rarely catch the attention of Human Rights groups in J&K.

The Army following a policy of 'Zero tolerance' against Human Rights violation, on the other hand, has been prompt in awarding strict punishments to its personnel who have in fact abberated from the strict rule of operation in counter insurgency situations be it in J&K or be it in the North East.

In the Army, it is ensured that punishment is metted out to erring personnel, unlike the police where conviction is rare and rarer still is the implementation of punishment. Army courts have issued a death sentence besides awarding rigorous imprisonments (RIs) of various durations to the proven guilty personnel and disbursed compensations to the tune of Rs 3,00,00 (three lakh) even to actual victims of Human Rights violations.

A glance at the state of allegations of Human Rights violation against the Army from 1994 to 2010 shows a distinct decrease in the number of cases. This has come about with an increased level of sensitivity amongst troops on human rights issues.

From the extensive interactions with troops as well as civilians in the Valley it would not be wrong to conclude that the institution of Human Rights has been blatantly misused by militants organisations and their sympathisers both within the state as well as outside it.

We have all to consider that unlike conventional operations, in CI and CT operations there are neither well defined boundaries nor a distinctly identifiable enemy. Most of the militants and the OGWs cannot be labeled as enemy since they are Indian nationals. But the feeling of the same brotherhood towards troops is lacking amongst many in the Valley. Troops are considered as outsiders and the Army an occupational force. No matter how good the Army behaves there is still a trust deficit which needs to be addressed. This trust deficit is more pronounced in the city centres rather than the remote villages.

Pockets such as Khiran, Sopore, Baramulla, Shopiyan and the Tral region which are known to be hardcore fundamentalist bases and dominated by Jamaatis are particularly anti-establishment and anti-Army/SF. Thus cooperation from the people in these places is the least.

The various problems faced by troops related to Human Rights in counter insurgency operations relate directly to the restrain they are required to exercise in population centres.

It can be understood that population control measures such as search and destroy operations, patrols, ambush etc cause inconvenience and disrupt routine life of a common man and aggrieves him, but it also needs to be understood that militants fully exploit the situation by using human shield tactics. There have been instances when militants have escaped from the backyard while people were resisting search parties. The resistance comes mostly from stone pelting women forming human chains or forming innovative threats of slapping Human Rights violation cases.

During 'contacts' with terrorists there are chances of collateral damage, though it is not a rule. This again is exploited by militants and their collaborators who do not leave a stone unturned in maligning the SF in the altar of Human Rights. Minor infringement on the part of the SF is scrutinised threadbare whereas gross violations of Human Rights by militants and their collaborators escape any kind of meaningful censure. To just say that militants are outlaws is giving them a license to carry on with their unlawful activities.

The seditious propaganda of using Human Rights as a tool is directed specifically against the SF thereby creating a rift between the local population and the SF. This compromises all efforts of the SF to nullify and eliminate militants and militancy and winning over the masses. Such propaganda also hampers the efforts of the Government and compels it to enforce further restrictions on the

SFs. The restrictions thus enforced, to avoid adverse publicity, only strengthens the militants and the sufferers are the SFs whose morale is affected. It acts as a dampener to those who are putting in their best, so that peace and normalcy is restored in the affected areas of the state.

It is seen that allegations of Human Rights violation labeled against the SFs is done only by a certain section of the population. This section behaves in the manner either under threat or fear of militants or, for the sake of money. They label false allegations against the SF and then send feelers asking for money to be paid to withdraw the Human Rights violation allegations.

The catch words 'Human Rights violation' are even used to threaten the SF now. Such allegations are resolved on the spot upon the undue payment of any sum of money.

The troops become over-cautious of Human Rights guidelines given to them, giving the militants and their sympathisers an opportunity to exploit this as a weakness.

The Centre has spent thousand of crores through the Army under Operation Sadhbhavna. This amount given to J&K is in addition to the Central budget for the state. This money has been spent in construction of schools, vocational training centres, mini-hydel projects, health care facilities, roads, stadia, orphanages etc. The Army's endeavour of 'winning the hearts and minds' of the people has well been accomplished, but it has not been given its due credit by many agencies, especially the media. It must be remembered that the Army acts only as an agency in spending the Centre's allocation to it for Operation Sadhbhavna and has to account for every penny that is spent.

The media, especially the vernacular press, has given exaggerated reports of violations of Human Rights to the people. It is found that a lot of media persons are not present at the site of the incident. Most of the times, the media reaches post incident and ends up interacting with sympathisers of the aggrieved, projecting the SF in poor light. Very few cases of militant atrocities have been reported in the media and there were hardly any follow up to cases reported. The control of some external force over the local media (print and electronic) cannot be ruled out all together seeing such biased reporting. It is also a possibility that the newspaper man is worried for his own safety, that if he is not sympathetic with militant organisations he may suddenly find himself on the 'hit list' of one or the other organisation. Thus the media mostly fails to be objective and unopinionated.

It is also the failure of the Army's media and HR management that it has not been able to prevail over the media houses and NGOs. The Army and other SF have not yet been able to (due to restraints on freedom of expression and communication) capitalise on the power and influence of the media. There has been a lack of pro-activism on the part of the Army when it comes of Human Rights and media management. Not to say that these organisations are sacrosanct.

It is interesting to note that Human Rights awareness is promoted not only by various training courses in the Army at the level of pre-commissioning training, young officers' courses, junior command courses but also by situational courses at the units which are assigned the task of supporting internal security duties or counter insurgency operations. The training extends to JCOs and other ranks as well. The troops are thoroughly sensitised on the tenets of Human Rights. Human Rights violation is not a policy or a practice by troops and abberations are misdeeds of individual men.

In evaluating the Human Rights record of the Army operating in J&K, one must take into account the unusual circumstances, inhospitable terrain, uncooperating and hostile local population, it is faced with. The psychological condition of a fatigued and stressed soldier in far off places, away from his family, operating in combat situations while facing the fear of the unknown need to be kept in mind. One must remember that Human Rights should not be restricted to only those few who can voice themselves but be the noble paradigm of all born human. Thus, by virtue it must bestow the same rights to a soldier. A soldier operating in trying circumstances, bound by a number of 'restrictive' rules and regulations is commonly outside in the gamut of the structure of Human Rights or so it appears. The AFSPA (which apparently is so 'anti-people') and the 'Commandments' put tremendous pressure on the soldier to perform without making mistakes.

The men operating in counter insurgency operations have strictly to adhere to the Commandments of the COAS and are aware of the consequences of abberating from any one of them. The Commandments serve as a compulsory precursor to all the operations and are based on the principles of Human Rights. Whereas, in reality the principles act as a dangerous restraint on any column which is in operation against militants who are not bound by any rule. For the militants every kill of a soldier gets them a booty and accolades.

We as a nation have conveniently forgotten the infamous Kunan Poshpora case(1991) of alleged rape of scores of women by troops, the butchering of Capt. Chauhan and Capt. Yadav into pieces by militants(1993) and mutilation and killing of Capt Sourabh Kalia and six of his men during the Kargil conflict(1999). These were the gravest violations of Human Rights of some soldiers – some humans – but all agencies alike preferred to be diplomatic and silent about them. Everybody liked to put it as 'hazards of the job'.

A civilian still has full rights to file something as basic as a defamation suit against anybody he thinks deserves to be questioned by law for defaming him, the same cannot be said of Army personnel or the Army as an institution. Of the cases proved false and baseless in favour of it in J&K, the Army has not claimed any damages from the alleging parties nor is it in a position to do that. Should it be permitted to claim some compensation for such false labeling of charges, then there will be for sure, a further reduction in the number of cases that are brought up, until absolutely genuine, against the Army.

The other fault line in the system can be seen in the state's treatment of violated persons. The state compensates civilian victims in case of loss of life, injuries caused etc in insurgency condition but has not done the same for any Army personnel so far. The solution of the problem lies in addressing the legislative mechanism that prompts such lopsided behaviour of the state. If constituent institutions of a society are to function smoothly for the welfare of the people, if they are to co-exist as functional units of the same human system, then they must extend their benefits to all and be answerable to the entire society that they aim to serve. The judiciary must equally be accessible to the Army man as much as it busies itself with those of the civilians and militants and their sympathisers. No one institution can be allowed to behave like a hegemon and this can happen only when their roles are made complementary rather than contradictory.

It is quite obvious that the people have now learnt the trick of the trade. They file allegations against SFs merely for obtaining monetary benefits. No matter how much Rights groups and civil societies demonstrate their angst demanding the withdrawal of the Army/SF, there are thousands more, especially in remote areas of J&K who do not favour such a proposition. They feel more threatened and harassed by militants and the state administration than by the presence of SFs. These are people who have benefitted from the Army's presence there, as also the developmental works undertaken by the Army which in the normal course should have been wholly and solely the concern of the state administration.

The Army has been used far too long in countering insurgency in Kashmir. The effects of which now manifest as counter-productive on both sides. The double jeopardy of fighting militants and showing restraint vide the Dos and Don'ts affects the morale of the troops, who perhaps sometimes fail to understand the reason they are there for. Fighting insurgency is not the business of the Army, for that purpose the State Police and Central Police Forces should be equipped. The Army cannot be expected to do policing and should be withdrawn. However, if the Army has to remain in such deployment and be operationally effective then the AFSPA which was promulgated in 1990 on a need basis, should stand minus any alterations.

The need of the hour is a better understanding of the AFSPA, its operational implications and the in-built accountability rather than giving in to the designs of militant/ insurgent groups and the political masters to repeal or dilute it. For whatever it might be, the Army HQ is atleast claiming to have punished 59 of its personnel including 22 officers, 4 JCOs and 33 other ranks in J&K from 1994 to 2010. The vagueness in the details of cases received and investigated (till the time of the work going to press) may be attributed to the fact that the HQ Cell in the Army HQ was established in 1993 whereas the Army has been in a state of deployment in J&K since 1990.

The ordinary people of Kashmir want peace, prosperity and development. They do not (at least any longer) ideologically support militants and militancy, but fail to stand united for the cause. The reason is not as much indifference, as is the fear of reprisal from hardliners and militants.

Nobody wants a terrorist in his backyard or be shot dead or beheaded and his cadaver hung on display. It is this fear of death that prevents people from being vocal about their disapproval for militancy and dislike of the inapt political handling of the matters of Kashmir.

Parties like the JKLF and APHC do not find ideological favour amongst the people. Their demonstration of strength is all bought over. People are paid or bullied to attend rallies. Rates are fixed even for stone pelting which go up to Rs.1000 (one thousand) depending on the difficulty level of the target. In Srinagar, where stone pelting has become an art for the youth, especially teenagers, an unemployed lad of bare 12-16 years of age can earn upto Rs. 2000 (two thousand) a month considering that the event takes place almost routinely after the Friday prayers in areas dominated by the JKLF and the moderate Hurriyat.

Foreign mercenaries who were once hailed as 'mehmaans' (guests) do not find favour with the local population any longer. This shift of attitude of the people has happened because of the brutal and intolerant ways of the foreign mercenaries. Beheadings, throat slitting and random killings of suspected informers, renegades or so called 'traitors' as also women, are the specialties of the foreign mercenaries.

The LET, HM and Al Badr are merciless when it comes to the control of foreign militants who are not willing to work for them. There is a lot of infight amongst the various Tanzeems and their operatives which the United Jihad Council covers under its aegis.

The people of Kashmir realise the futility of militancy and violence and now local boys rarely cross over to POK to receive arms training. This realisation has also dawned because of the comparative study made by former militants and erstwhile aspirants, of life and life style on both sides of the LOC.

The concepts of 'Jihad' and 'Azaadi' are sold only to a few who are willing to buy it for personal benefits. The vested interests of both the buyer and the seller is known to the ordinary people of Kashmir. But it is the voice of these ordinary people that is suppressed by instilling fear in them. The election results of the Parliament, the State Assembly and more recently the Panchayat should be taken as signs of what actually the people of Kashmir aspire for. The purchasing power of money coupled with dirty politics is responsible for ruining generations of Kashmiris.

Sources in Kashmir based civil society had claimed that there is a lot of anger presently in the people of Kashmir and that their demand is freedom – 'Azaadi'. This is quite a contradiction with what the same people of Kashmir had to opine during interactions with the author. As mentioned earlier their support to mass movements such as protest rallies, bandhs and stone peltings, are primarily bought over or carried out, out of fear. The lurking danger in Kashmir is this untamed anger especially of the youth in Kupwara, Srinagar, Sopore, Anantnag, Pulwama and Shopiyan areas which is a potent tool in the hands of fundamentalist and separatists.

One has also to consider that these areas excepting Srinagar are primarily Jamaati influenced with the PDP having made deep inroads too. The frequent uprising (a summer phenomenon) and the proportion to which this so called 'anger' escalates could well be a resurgence of the cycle of violence witnessed in the 1980s, followed by an armed struggle and then the de-escalation if not effectively nipped in the bud. If the resurgence factor be true then this time round it is going to be much more difficult an affair to tackle by New Delhi with all its forces, as the Kashmiri people are much more aware, funded and have evolved in carrying their 'struggle' ahead.

It must be understood that food, shelter and clothing are not at the core of the Kashmiri peoples struggle – cry for the right to self determination does not usually come out of hungry stomachs. Nobody in Kashmir goes hungry (meat is the preferred dietary inclusion), there are no beggars, nobody dies in the freezing cold.

Compare this with the lesser lucky people of Bihar, Orissa, Uttar Pradesh and the likes. The Centre is giving enough money to keep every stomach filled in the Valley, has been doing so and perhaps will continue to do so to appease them. Perhaps for a certain section of the Kashmiri people this too is a well drawn strategy – to drain the Centre monetarily if not militarily.

Not all Kashmiris identify themselves as an integral part of India. Fuelling the fire and nurturing the seeds of dissent may hot only be the interest of Pakistan but western powers as well considering the geo-political interests of their countries in the region. Not to forget the presence of the 'dragon' so close home.

The prevailing militancy environment in Kashmir is multi-dimensional for India, as it spans across a proxy war, dissent of the people, political differences and the tangle over key issues such as dilution of Article 370 and autonomy. If after sixty four years of Independence and acceptance of 'sovereign' rule, only one state continues to be accepted as 'special' (vide Article 370 of the Constitution) then it must be admitted that ideally injustice is being done to the rest of the federating units of the country.

The Valley will simmer so long as a political solution is not arrived at, and violations will continue to haunt the Armed Forces for as long as they are engaged in countering what otherwise has a political genesis.

It should not be forgotten that the politics of Human Rights has been historically endemic to cities in Kashmir where ideologues, elites and intellectuals join forces pretending as the only voice of the entire population. Much of the attention that such cells (often inspired and funded by agencies worldwide) draw, is through a 'systemic' non observation of the violence caused by those they seek to protect or represent. In remote undeveloped villages these Rights' activists, NGOs etc do not bother to grace people with their concern. Their 'genuine' interests in raising peoples' awareness or creating modes of dialogue or simply helping people live with dignity is itself a city centric, capital centric, politically motivated propaganda which is beyond national boundaries.

The persistence of such NGOs and Rights groups to highlight only those incidents that fit their theory is pathological to an extent that they (i.e the so called upholders of 'Human' Rights) end up completely de humanising the losses, humiliations, deaths of the 'other' (ref : IPTK report Pg 2, Buried Evidence). They like to conveniently ignore circumstantial evidences of militant atrocities and paralise the judicial apparatus.

Here it is argued that 'other' (that is the Armed Forces) is not a monolithic entity which should invariably lead us to think of it as an oppressed lot. The military is as much an 'other' as the populace and should be entitled to equal Human Rights.

Fatalities in Terrorist Violence 1988 - 2011

	Incidents	Civilians	Security Force Personnel	Terrorists	Total
1988	390	29	1	1	31
1989	2154	79	13	0	92
1990	3905	862	132	183	1177
1991	3122	594	185	614	1393
1992	4971	859	177	873	1909
1993	4457	1023	216	1328	2567
1994	4484	1012	236	1651	2899
1995	4479	1161	297	1338	2796
1996	4224	1333	376	1194	2903
1997	3004	840	355	1177	2372
1998	2993	877	339	1045	2261
1999	2938	799	555	1184	2538
2000	2835	842	638	1808	3288
2001	3278	1067	590	2850	4507
2002	NA	839	469	1714	3022
2003	NA	658	338	1546	2542
2004	NA	534	325	951	1810
2005	NA	521	218	1000	1739
2006	NA	349	168	599	1116
2007	NA	164	121	492	777
2008	NA	69	90	382	541
2009	NA	55	78	242	375
2010	NA	36	69	270	375
2011	NA	27	15	59	101
Total*	47234	14629	6001	22501	43131

Data till July 24, 2011*

Annexure 2

The Gazette of India

Extraordinary

Part II-Section 1

Published by Authority

New Delhi, Tuesday, September 11, 1990/ Bhadra 20, 1912

Ministry of Law and Justice

(Legislative Department)

New Delhi, the 11th September, 1990/Bhadra 20, 1912 *(Saka)*

The following Act of Parliament received the assent of the President on the 10th September 1990, and is hereby published for general information:

The Armed Forces (Jammu and Kashmir Special Powers Act, 1990

No. 21 OF 1990

[10th September, 1990.]

An Act to enable certain special powers to be conferred upon members of the armed forces in the disturbed areas in the State of Jammu and Kashmir.

Be it enacted by Parliament in the Forty-first Year of the Republic of India as follows:-

1. Short title, extent and commencement :-

(a) This Act may be called the Armed Forces (Jammu and Kashmir) Special Powers Act, 1990.

(b) It extends to the whole of the State of Jammu and Kashmir.

(c) It shall be deemed to have come into force on the 5th day of July, 1990.

2. Definitions. In this Act, unless the context otherwise requires —

(a) "armed forces" means the military forces and the air forces operating as land forces and includes any other armed forces of the Union so operating

(b) "disturbed area" means an area which is for the time being declared by notification under section 3 to be a disturbed area;

(c) all other words and expressions 'used herein, but not defined and defined in the Air Force Act, 19501, or the Army Act, 1950, shall have the meanings respectively assigned to them in those Acts.

3. Power to declare areas to be disturbed areas.

If, in relation to the State of Jammu and Kashmir, the Governor of that State or the Central Government, is of opinion that the whole or any part of the State is in such a disturbed and dangerous condition that the use of armed forces in aid of the civil power is necessary to prevent—

(a) activities involving terrorist acts directed towards overawing the Government as by law established or striking terror in the people or any section of the people or alienating any section of the people or adversely affecting the harmony amongst different sections of the people;

(b) activities directed towards disclaiming, questioning or disrupting the sovereignty and territorial integrity of India or bringing about cession of a part of the territory of India or secession of a part of the territory of India front the Union or causing insult to the Indian National Flag, the Indian National Anthem and the Constitution of India, the Governor of the State or the Central Government, may, by notification in the Official Gazette, declare the whole *or* any part of the State to be a disturbed area.

Explanation.- In this section, "terrorist act" has the same meaning as in *Explanation* to article 248 of the Constitution of India as applicable to the State of Jammu and Kashmir.

4. Special powers of the armed forces.

Any commissioned officer, warrant officer, non-commissioned officer or any other person of equivalent rank in the armed forces may, in a disturbed area,-

(a) if he is of opinion that it is necessary so to do for the maintenance of public order, after giving such due warning as he may consider necessary, fire upon or otherwise use force, even to the causing of death, against any person who is acting in contravention of any law or order for the time being in force in the disturbed area prohibiting the assembly of five or more persons or the carrying of weapons or of things capable of being used as weapons or of firearms, ammunition or explosive substances;

(b) if he is of opinion that it is necessary so to do, destroy any arms dump, prepared or fortified position or shelter from which armed attacks are made or are likely to be made or are attempted to be made, or any structure used as training camp for armed volunteers or utilized as a hide-out by armed gangs or absconders wanted for any offence;

(c) arrest, without warrant, any persons who has committed a cognizable offence or against whom a reasonable suspicion exists that he has committed or is about to commit a cognizable offence and may use such force as may be necessary to effect the arrest;

(d) enter and search, without warrant, any premises to make any such arrest as aforesaid or to recover any person believed to be wrongful restrained or confined or any property reasonably suspected to be stolen property or any arms, ammunition or explosive substances believed to be unlawful kept in such premises, and may for that purpose use such force as may be necessary, and seize any such property, arms, ammunition or explosive substances;

(e) stop, search and seize any vehicle or vessel reasonably suspected to be carrying any person who is a proclaimed offender, or any persons who has committed a non-cognizable offence, or against whom a reasonable suspicion exists that he has committed or is about to commit a non-cognizable offence, or any person who is carrying any arms, ammunition or explosive substance believed to be unlawfully held by him, and may, for that purpose, use such force as may be necessary to effect such stoppage, search or seizure, as the case may be.

5. Power of search to include powers to break open locks, etc.

Every person making a search under this Act shall have the power to break open the lock of any door, almirah, safe, box, cupboard, drawer, package or other thing, if the key thereof is withheld.

6. Arrested persons and seized property to be made over to the police.

Any person arrested and taken into custody under this Act and every property, arms, ammunition or explosive substance or any vehicle or vessel seized under this Act, shall be made over to the officer-incharge of the nearest police station with the least possible delay, together with a report of the circumstances occasioning the arrest, or as the case may be, occasioning the seizure of such property, arms, ammunition or explosive substance or any vehicle or vessel, as the case may be.

7. Protection of persons acting in good faith under this Act.

No prosecution, suit or other legal proceeding shall be instituted, except with the previous sanction of the Central Government, against any person in respect of anything done or purported to be done in exercise of the powers conferred by this Act.

8. Repeal and saving –

(1) The Armed Forces (Jammu and Kashmir) Special Powers Ordinance, 1990[3], is hereby repealed.

(2) Notwithstanding such repeal, anything done or any action taken under the said Ordinance shall be deemed to have been done or taken under the corresponding provisions of this Act.

V.S. RAMA DEVI,
Secy. to the Govt. of India

Corrigenda

In the Constitution (Sixty-sixth Amendment) Act, 1990 as published in the Gazette of India, Extraordinary, Part II, Section 1, dated the 7th June, 1990 (Issue No.32),-

At page 1, in second line from the bottom, for "Regulation, 1963 (Andhra Pradesh Regulation 2 of" read "Regulation, 1970 (Andhra Pradesh Regulation 1 of".

At page 2, in line 7, for "(Bihar Act 8 of 1985)" reads "(Bihar Act 8 of 1885)".

---

1 45 of 1950

2 46 of 1990

3 3 of 1990

Extraordinary

The Jammu & Kashmir Government Gazette

Vol. 103] Srinagar, Fri., the 6th July, 90/15th Asa., 1912. [No.14-1

PART I-B

Jammu and Kashmir Government – Notifications.

Government of Jammu and Kashmir, Civil Secretariat -Home Department

SRO NO. SW 4   Dated 6-7, 1990

In exercise of the powers conferred under section 3 of the Armed Forces (Jammu and Kashmir) Special Powers Ordinance, 1990, the Governor of Jammu and Kashmir hereby notifies the areas given in the Schedule to this notification as Disturbed Areas.

(Sd.)……………………………….
Additional Chief Secretary (Home),
Jammu and Kashmir Government

Schedule

1. Areas falling within 20 Kms. of the Line of Control in the Districts of Rajouri and Poonch.

2. Districts of Anangtnag, Baramulla, Badgam, Kupwara, Pulwama and Srinagar.

(Sd)...
Additional Chief Secretary (Home),
Jammu and Kashmir Government.

Government of Jammu and Kashmir
Civil Secretariat Home Department

Notification

Srinagar, The 10 Thausugt, 2001

SRO 351: Whereas the Governor is of the opinion that the State is in such a disturbed condition that the use of Armed Forces in the aid of civil power is necessary to prevent the activities involving terrorists acts directed towards striking terror in the people;

Now, therefore, in exercise of the powers conferred by section 3 of the Armed Forces (Jammu and Kashmir) Special Powers Act, 1990, the Governor hereby declares the districts of Jammu, Kathu, Udhampur, Poonch, Rajouri and Doda to be disturbed areas in addition to districts, Srinagar, Budgam, Anantnag, Pulwama, Baramulla and Kupwara which stand already so declared.

By order of the Governor

Principal Secretary to Government
Home Department

NO:Home-219/97-ISA

dated 10.8.2001.

Copy for information to:-

1. Chief Secretary, J&K, Srinagar.

2. Secretary, Ministry of Home Affairs, Govt. of India, New Delhi.

3. Secretary, Ministry of Defence, Govt. of India, New Delhi.

4. Joint Secretary (K-I), MHA (Deptt. of J&K Affairs), New Delhi.

5. Principal Secretary to HE the Governor.

6. Principal Secretary to Hon'ble Chief Minister.

7. Commr/Secretary, Law.

8. Director General Police, Srinagar.

9. Director General, BSF, New Delhi.

10. Director General, ITBP, New Delhi.

11. Director General, CRPF, New Delhi.

12. GOC, XVI Corps C/o 56 APO

13. GOC, XV Corps C/o 56 APO

14. GOC, XIV Corps C/o 56 APO

15. Divisional Commissioner, Jammu.

16. Director Information, J&K, Srinagar.

17. All District Magistrates of Jammu Division.

18. All District Superintendents of Police, Jammu Division.

19. Pvt. Secretary to Hon'ble MOS(Home)

Annexure 3

Human Right Act 1993

An Act to provide for the constitution of a National Human Rights Commission. State Human Rights Commission in States and Human Rights Courts for better protection of Human Rights and for matters connected therewith or incidental thereto.

Be it enacted by the parliament in the forty-fourth year of the Republic of India as follows-

Chapter I   Preliminary

Chapter II   The National Human Rights Commission

Chapter III   Functions and Powers of the Commission

Chapter VI   Procedure

Chapter V   State Human Rights Commissions

Chapter VI   Human Rights Courts

Chapter VII   Finance, Accounts and Audit

Chapter VIII   Miscellaneous

Chapter I

Preliminary

Short title, extent and commencement

(a) This Act may be called the Protection of Human Rights Act, 1993.

(b) It extends to the whole of India. Provided that it shall apply to the State of Jammu and Kashmir only in so far as it pertains to the matters relatable to any of the entries enumerated in List I or List lll in the Seventh Schedule to the Constitution as applicable to that State.

(c) It shall be deemed to have come into force on the 28th day of September, 1993.

Definitions

In this Act, unless the context otherwise requires-

(a) "armed forces" means the naval, military and air forces and includes any other armed forces of the Union;

(b) "Chairperson" means the Chairperson of the Commission or of the State Commission, as the case may be;

(c) "Commission" means the National Human Rights Commission under section

(d) "human rights" means the rights relating to life, liberty, cquality and dignity of the individual guaranteed by the Constitution or embodied in the International Covenants and enforceable by courts in India.

(e) "Human Rights Court" means the Human Rights Court specified under section 30;

(f) "International Covenants" means the International Covenant on Civil and Political Rights and the International Covenant on Economic, Social and Cultural Rights adopted by the General Assembly of the United Nations on the 16th December, 1966;

(g) "Member" means a Member of the Commission or of the State Commission, as the case may be, and includes the Chairperson;

(h) "National Commission for Minorities" means the National Commission for Minorities constituted under section 3 of the National Commission for Minorities Act, 1992;

(j) "National Commission for the Scheduled Castes and Scheduled Tribes" means the National Commission for the Scheduled Castes and Scheduled Tribes referred to in article 338 of the Constitution;

(k) "National Commission for Women" means the National Commission for Women constituted under section 3 of the National Commission for Women Act, 1990;

(l) "Notification" means a notification published in the official Gazette;

(m) "Prescribed" means prescribed by rules made under this Act;

(n) "Public servant" shall have the meaning assigned to it in section 21 of the Indian Penal Code;

(o) "State Commission" means a State Human Rights Commission constituted under section 21.

Any reference in this Act to a law, which is not in force in the State of Jammu and Kashmir, shall, in relation to that State, be construed as a reference to a corresponding law, if any, in force in that State.

Chapter II

The National Human Rights Commission

Constitution of a National Human Rights Commission

(1) The Central Government shall constitute a body to be known as the National Human Rights Commission to exercise the powers conferred upon, and to perform the functions assigned to it, under this Act.

(2) The Commission shall consist of:

    (a) a Chairperson who has been a Chief Justice of the Supreme Court;

    (b) one Member who is or has been, a Judge of the Supreme Court;

    (c) one Member who is, or has been, the Chief Justice of a High Court;

    (d) two Members to be appointed from amongst persons having knowledge of, or practical experience in, matters relating to human rights.

(3) The Chairpersons of the National Commission for Minorities, the National Commission for the Scheduled Castes and Scheduled Tribes and the National Commission for Women shall be deemed to be Members of the Commission for the discharge of functions specified in clauses (b) to (j) of section 12.

(4) There shall be a Secretary-General who shall be the Chief Executive Officer of the Commission and shall exercise such powers and discharge such functions of the Commission as it may delegate to him.

(5) The headquarters of the Commission shall be at Delhi and the Commission may, with the previous approval of the Central Government, establish offices at other places in India.

Appointment of Chairperson and other Members

(1)   The Chairperson and other Members shall be appointed by the President by warrant under his hand and seal.

Provided that every appointment under this sub-section shall be made after obtaining the recommendations of a Committee consisting of

(a)   The Prime Minister —Chairperson

(b)   Speaker of the House of the People — Member

(c)   Minister in-charge of the Ministry of Home Affairs in the Government of India — Member

(d)   Leader of the Opposition in the House of the People — Member

(e)   Leader of the Opposition in the Council of States — Member

(f)   Deputy Chairman of the Council of States — Member

Provided further that no sitting Judge of the Supreme Court or sitting Chief Justice of a High Court shall be appointed except after consultation with the Chief Justice of India.

(2) No appointment of a Chairperson or a Member shall be invalid merely by reason of any vacancy in the Committee.

Removal of a Member of the Commission

(1) Subject to the provisions of sub-section (2), the Chairperson or any other Member of the Commission shall only be removed from his office by order of the President on the ground of proved misbehaviour or incapacity after the Supreme Court, on reference being made to it by the President, has, on inquiry held in accordance with the procedure prescribed in that behalf by the Supreme Court, reported that the Chairperson or such other Member, as the case may be, ought on any such ground to be removed.

(2) Notwithstanding anything in sub-section (1), the President may by order remove from office the Chairperson or any other Member if

the Chairperson or such other Member, as the case may be

(a) is adjudged an insolvent; or

(b) engages during his term of office in any paid employment out side the duties of his office: or

(c) is unfit to continue in office by reason of infirmity of mind or body; or

(d) is of unsound mind and stands so declared by a competent court; or

(e) is convicted and sentenced to imprisonment for an offence which in the opinion of the President involves moral turpitude.

Term of office of Members

(1) A person appointed as Chairperson shall hold office for a term of five years from the date on which he enters upon his office or until he attains the age of seventy years, whichever is earlier.

(2) A person appointed as a Member shall hold office for a term of five years from the date on which he enters upon his office and shall be eligible for re-appointment for another term of five years. Provided that no Member shall hold office after he has attained the age of seventy years.

(3) On ceasing to hold office, a Chairperson or a Member shall be ineligible for further employment under the Government of India or under the Government of any State.

Member to act as Chairperson or to discharge his functions in certain circumstances

(1) In the event of the occurrence of any vacancy in the office of the Chairperson by reason of his death, resignation or otherwise, the President may, by notification, authorise one of the Members to act as the Chairperson until the appointment of a new Chairperson to fill such vacancy.

(2) When the Chairperson is unable to discharge his functions owing to

absence on leave or otherwise, such one of the Members as the President may, by notification, authorise in this behalf, shall discharge the functions of the Chairperson until the date on which the Chairperson resumes his duties.

Terms and conditions of service of Members

The salaries and allowances payable to, and other terms and conditions of service of, the Members shall be such as may be prescribed. Provided that neither the salary and allowances nor the other terms and conditions of service of a Member shall be varied to his disadvantage after his appointment.

Vacancies, etc., not to invalidate the proceedings of the Commission.

No act or proceedings of the Commission shall be questioned or shall be invalidated merely on the ground of existence of any vacancy or defect in the constitution of the Commission.

Procedure to be regulated by the Commission

(1) The Commission shall meet at such time and place as the Chairperson may think fit.

(2) The Commission shall regulate its own procedure.

(3) All orders and decisions of the Commission shall be audited by the Secretary-General or any other officer of the Commission duly authorised by the Chairperson in this behalf.

Officers and other staff of the Commission

(1) The Central Government shall make available to the Commission :

(a) an officer of the rank of the Secretary to the Government of India who shall be the Secretary-General of the Commission; and

(b) such police and investigative staff under an officer not below the rank of a Director General of Police and such other offic ers and staff as may be necessary for the efficient perfor mance of the functions of the Commission.

(2) Subject to such rules as may be made by the Central Government in this behalf, the Commission may appoint such other administrative, technical and scientific staff as it may consider necessary.

(3) The salaries, allowances and conditions of service of the officers and other staff appointed under sub-section (2) shall be such as may be prescribed.

Chapter III
Function and Powers of the Commission

Functions of the Commission

The Commission shall perform all or any of the following functions, namely :

(a) inquire, suo motu or on a petition presented to it by a victim or any person on his behalf, into complaint of

(i) violation of human rights or abetment thereof or

(ii) negligence in the prevention of such violation, by a public servant;

(b) intervene in any proceeding involving any allegation of violation of human rights pending before a court with the approval of such court;

(c) visit, under intimation to the State Government, any jail or any other institution under the control of the State Government, where persons are detained or lodged for purposes of treatment, reformation or protection to study the living conditions of the inmates and make recommendations thereon;

(d) review the safeguards provided by or under the Constitution or any law for the time being in force for the protection of human rights and recommend measures for their effective implementation;

(e) review the factors, including acts of terrorism that inhibit the enjoyment of human rights and recommend appropriate remedial measures;

(f) study treaties and other international instruments on human rights and make recommendations for their effective implementation;

(g) undertake and promote research in the field of human rights;

(h) spread human rights literacy among various sections of society and promote awareness of the safeguards available for the protection of these rights through publications, the media, seminars and other available means;

(j) encourage the efforts of non-governmental organisations and institutions working in the field of human rights;

(k) such other functions as it may consider necessary for the protection of human rights.

Powers relating to inquiries

(1) The Commission shall, while inquiring into complaints under this Act, have all the powers of a civil court trying a suit under the Code of Civil Procedure, 1908, and in particular in respect of the following matters, namely :

    (a) summoning and enforcing the attendance of witnesses and ex amine them on oath;

    (b) discovery and production of any document;

    (c) receiving evidence on affidavits;

    (d) requisitioning any public record or copy thereof from any court or office;

    (e) issuing commissions for the examination of witnesses or docu ments;

    (f) any other matter which may be prescribed.

(2) The Commission shall have power to require any person, subject to any privilege which may be claimed by that person under any law for the time being in force, to furnish information on such points or matters as, in the opinion of the Commission, may be useful for, or relevant to, the subject matter of the inquiry and any person so required shall be deemed to be legally bound to furnish such information within the meaning of section 176 and section 177 of the Indian Penal Code.

(3) The Commission or any other officer, not below the rank of a Gazetted Officer, specially authorised in this behalf by the Commission may enter any building or place where the Commission has reason to believe that any document relating to the subject

matter of the inquiry may be found, and may seize any such document or take extracts or copies therefrom subject to the provisions of section 100 of the Code of Criminal Procedure, 1973, in so far as it may be applicable.

(4) The Commission shall be deemed to be a civil court and when any offence as is described in section 175, section 178, section 179, section 180 or section 228 of the Indian Penal Code is committed in the view or presence of the Commission, the Commission may, after recording the facts constituting the

offence and the statement of the accused as provided for in the Code of Criminal Procedure, 1973, forward the case to a Magistrate having jurisdiction to try the same and the Magistrate to whom any such case is forwarded shall proceed to hear the complaint against the accused as if the case has been forwarded to him under section 346 of the Code of Criminal Procedure, 1973.

(5) Every proceeding before the Commission shall be deemed to be a judicial proceeding within the meaning of sections 193 and 228, and for the purposes of section 196, of the Indian Penal Code, and the Commission shall be deemed to be a civil court for all the purposes of section 195 and Chapter XXVI of the Code of Criminal Procedure, 1973.

Investigation

(1) The Commission may, for the purpose of conducting any investigation pertaining to the inquiry, utilise the services of any officer or investigation agency of the Central Government or any State Government with the concurrence of the Central Government or the State Government, as the case may be.

(2) For the purpose of investigating into any matter pertaining to the inquiry, any officer or agency whose services are utilised under sub-section (1) may, subject to the direction and control of the Commission.

   (a) summon and enforce the attendance of any person and ex amine him;

    (b) require the discovery and production of any document; and

    (c) requisition any public record or copy thereof from any of fice.

(3) The provisions of section 15 shall apply in relation to any statement made by a person before any officer or agency whose services are utilised under sub-section (1) as they apply in relation to any statement made by a person in the course of giving evidence before the Commission.

(4) The officer or agency whose services are utilised under sub-section (1) shall investigate into any matter pertaining to the inquiry and submit a report thereon to the Commission within such period as may be specified by the Commission in this behalf.

(5) The Commission shall satisfy itself about the correctness of the facts stated and the conclusion, if any, arrived at in the report subbed to it under sub-section (4) and for this purpose the Commission may make such inquiry (including the examination of the person or persons who conducted or assisted in the investigation) as it thinks fit.

Statement made by persons to the Commission

No statement made by a person in the course of giving evidence before the Commission shall subject him to, or be used against him in, any civil or criminal proceeding except a prosecution for giving false evidence by such statement:

Provided that the statement —

    (a) is made in reply to the question which he is required by the Commission to answer; or

    (b) is relevant to the subject matter of the inquiry.

Persons likely to be prejudicially affected to be heard

  If, at any stage of the inquiry, the Commission-

    (a) considers it necessary to inquire into the conduct of any person; or

(b) is of the opinion that the reputation of any person is likely to be prejudicially affected by the inquiry; it shall give to that person a reasonable opportunity of being heard in the inquiry and to produce evidence in his defence:

Provided that nothing in this section shall apply where the credit of a witness is being impeached.

Chapter IV
Procedure

Inquiry into complaints

The Commission while inquiring into the complaints of violations of human rights may-

    (i) call for information or report from the Central Government or any State Government or any other authority or organisation subordinate thereto within such time as may be specified by it;

Provided that-

    (a) if the information or report is not received within the time stipulated by the Commission, it may proceed to inquire into the complaint on its own;

    (b) if, on receipt of information or report, the Commission is satisfied either that no further inquiry is required or that the required action has been initiated or taken by the concerned Government or authority, it may not proceed with the complaint and inform the complainant accordingly;

    (ii) without prejudice to anything contained in clause (i), if it considers necessary, having regard to the nature of the complaint, initiate an inquiry.

Steps after inquiry

The Commission may take any of the following steps upon the completion of an inquiry held under this Act namely :

    (1) where the inquiry discloses, the commission of violation of human rights or negligence in the prevention of violation of human rights by a public servant, it may recommend to the concerned Government or authority the initiation of proceedings for prosecution or such other action as the Commission may deem fit against the concerned person or persons;

    (2) approach the Supreme Court or the High Court concerned for such

directions, orders or writs as that Court may deem necessary;

(3) recommend to the concerned Government or authority for the grant of such immediate interim relief to the victim or the members of his family as the Commission may consider necessary;

(4) subject to the provisions of clause (5), provide a copy of the inquiry report to the petitioner or his representative;

(5) the Commission shall send a copy of its inquiry report together with its recommendations to the concerned Government or authority and the concerned Government or authority shall, within a period of one month, or such further time as the Commission may allow, forward its comments on the report, including the action taken or proposed to be taken thereon, to the Commission;

(6) the Commission shall publish its inquiry report together with the comments of the concerned Government or authority, if any, and the action taken or proposed to be taken by the concerned Government or authority on the recommendations of the Commission.

Procedure with respect to armed forces

(1) Notwithstanding anything contained in this Act, while dealing with complaints of violation of human rights by members of the armed forces, the Commission shall adopt the following procedure, namely :

(a) it may, either on its own motion or on receipt of a petition, seek a report from the Central Government;

(b) after the receipt of the report, it may, either not proceed with the complaint or, as the case may be, make its recommendations to that Government.

(2) The Central Government shall inform the Commission of the action taken on the recommendations within three months or such further time as the Commission may allow.

(3) The Commission shall publish its report together with its recommendations made to the Central Government and the action

taken by that Government on such recommendations.

(4) The Commission shall provide a copy of the report published under sub-section (3) to the petitioner or his representative.

Annual and special reports of the Commission

(1) The Commission shall submit an annual report to the Central Government and to the State Government concerned and may at any time submit special reports on any matter which, in its opinion, is of such urgency or importance that it should not be deferred till submission of the annual report.

(2) The Central Government and the State Government, as the case may be, shall cause the annual and special reports of the Commission to be laid before each House of Parliament or the State Legislature respectively, as the case may be, along with a memorandum of action taken or proposed to be taken on the recommendations of the Commission and the reasons for non-acceptance of the recommendations, if any.

Chapter V
State Human Rights Commissions

Constitution of State Human Rights Commissions

(1) A State Government may constitute a body to be known as the .... (name of the State) Human Rights Commission to exercise the powers conferred upon, and to perform the functions assigned to, a State Commission under this chapter.

(2) The State Commission shall consist of

    (a)   a Chairperson who has been a Chief Justice of a High Court;

    (b)   one Member who is, or has been, a Judge of a High Court;

    (c)   one Member who is, or has been, a district judge in that State;

    (d)   two Members to be appointed from amongst persons having knowledge of, or practical experience in, matters relating to human rights.

(3) There shall be a Secretary who shall be the Chief Executive Officer of the State Commission and shall exercise such powers and discharge such functions of the State Commission as it may delegate to him.

(4) The headquarters of the State Commission shall be at such place as the State Government may, by notification, specify.

(5) A State Commission may inquire into violation of human rights only in respect of matters relatable to any of the entries enumerated in List II and List III in the Seventh Schedule to the Constitution:

Provided that if any such matter is already being inquired into by the Commission or any other Commission duly constituted under any law for the time being in force, the State Commission shall not inquire into the said matter:

Provided further that in relation to the Jammu and Kashmir Human Rights Commission, this sub-section shall have effect as if for the words and figures "List II and List III in the Seventh Schedule to the Constitution", the words and figures "List III in the Seventh Schedule to the Constitution as applicable to the State of Jammu and Kashmir and in respect of matters in relation to which the Legislature of that State has power to make laws" had been substituted.

Appointment of Chairperson and other Members of State Commission

(1) The Chairperson and other Members shall be appointed by the Governor by warrant under his hand and seal:

Provided that every appointment under this sub-section shall be made after obtaining the recommendation of a Committee consisting of

(a) the Chief Minister — Chairperson

(b) Speaker of the Legislative Assembly — Member

(c) Minister in-charge of the Department of Home, in that State — Member

(d) Leader of the Opposition in the Legislative Assembly — Member

Provided further that where there is a Legislative Council in a State, the Chairman of that Council and the Leader of the Opposition in that Council shall also be members of the Committee.

Provided also that no sitting Judge of a High Court or a sitting District Judge shall be appointed except after consultation with the Chief Justice of the High Court of the concerned State.

(2) No appointment of a Chairperson or a Member of the State Commission shall be invalid merely by reason of any vacancy in the Committee.

Removal of a Member of the State Commission

(1) Subject to the provisions of sub-section (2), the Chairperson or any other member of the State Commission shall only be removed from his office by order of the President on the ground of proved misbehaviour or incapacity after the Supreme Court, on a reference being made to it by the President, has, on inquiry held in accordance with the procedure prescribed in that behalf by the Supreme Court, reported that the Chairperson or such other Member, as the case

may be, ought on any such ground to be removed.

(2) Notwithstanding anything in sub-section (1), the President may by order remove from office the Chairperson or any other Member if the Chairperson or such other Member, as the case may be –

(a) is adjudged an insolvent; OR

(b) engages during his term of office in any paid employment outside the duties of his office; OR

(c) is unfit to continue in office by reason of infirmity of mind or body; OR

(d) is of unsound mind and stands so declared by a competent court; OR

(e) is convicted and sentenced to imprisonment for an offence which in the opinion of the President involves moral turpitude.

Term of office of Members of the State Commission

(1) A person appointed as Chairperson shall hold office for a term of five years from the date on which he enters upon his office or until he attains the age of seventy years, whichever is earlier;

(2) A person appointed as a Member shall hold office for a term of five years from the date on which he enters upon his office and shall be eligible for re-appointment for another term of five years;

Provided that no Member shall hold office after he has attained the age of seventy years.

(3) On ceasing to hold office, a Chairperson or a Member shall be ineligible for further employment under the Government of a State or under the Government of India.

Member to act as Chairperson or to discharge his func tions in certain circumstances

(1) In the event of the occurrence of any vacancy in the office of the Chairperson by reason of his death, resignation or otherwise, the Governor may, by notification, authorise one of the Members to act as the Chairperson until the appointment of a new Chairperson to

fill such vacancy.

(2) When the Chairperson is unable to discharge his functions owing to absence on leave or otherwise, such one of the Members as the Governor may, by notification, authorise in this behalf, shall discharge the functions of the Chairperson until the date on which the Chairperson resumes his duties.

Terms and conditions of service of Members of the State Commission

The salaries and allowances payable to, and other terms and conditions of service of, the Members shall be such as may be prescribed by the State Government.

Provided that neither the salary and allowances nor the other terms and conditions of service of a Member shall be varied to his disadvantage after his appointment.

Officers and other staff of the State Commission

(1) The State Government shall make available to the Commission

(a) an officer not below the rank of a Secretary to the State Government who shall be the Secretary of the State Commission; and

(b) such police and investigative staff under an officer not below the rank of an Inspector General of Police and such other officers and staff as may be necessary for the efficient performance of the functions of the State Commission.

(2) subject to such rules as may be made by the State Government in this behalf, the State Commission may appoint such other administrative, technical and scientific staff as it may consider necessary.

(3) The salaries, allowances and conditions of service of the officers and other staff appointed under sub-section (2) shall be such as may be prescribed by the State Government.

Annual and special reports of State Commission

(1) The State Commission shall submit an annual report to the State

Government and may at any time submit special reports on any matter which, in its opinion, is of such urgency or importance that it should not be deferred till submission of the annual report.

(2) The State Government shall cause the annual and special reports of the State Commission to be laid before each House of State Legislature where it consists of two Houses, or where such Legislature consists of one House, before that House along with a memorandum of action taken or proposed to be taken on the recommendations of the State Commission and the reasons for non-acceptance of the rections, if any.

Application of certain provisions relating to National Human Rights Commission to State Commissions

The provisions of sections 9, 10, 12, 13, 14, 15, 16, 17 and 18 shall apply to a State Commission and shall have effect, subject to the following modifications, namely :-

(a) references to "Commission" shall be construed as refer ences to "State Commission";

(b) In section 10, in sub-section (3), for the word "Secretary General", the word "Secretary" shall be substituted;

(c) in section 12, clause (f) shall be omitted;

(d) in section 17, in clause (i), the words "Central Government or any" shall be omitted;

Chapter VI
Human Rights Courts

For the purpose of providing speedy trial of offences arising out of violation of human rights, the State

Government may, with the concurrence of the Chief Justice of the High Court, by notification, specify for each district a Court of Session to be a Human Rights Court to try the said offences.

Provided that nothing in this section shall apply if

(a)   a Court of Session is already specified as a special court; or

(b)   a special court is already constituted, for such offences under any other law for the time being in force.

Special Public Prosecutor

For every Human Rights Court, the State Government shall, by notification, specify a Public Prosecutor or appoint an advocate who has been in practice as an advocate for not less than seven years, as a Special Public Prosecutor for the purpose of conducting cases in that Court.

Chapter VII
Finance, Accounts and Audit

Grants by the Central Government

(1) The Central Government shall after due appropriation made by Parliament by law in this behalf, pay to the Commission by way of grants such sums of money as the Central Government may think fit for being utilised for the purposes of this Act.

(2) The Commission may spend such sums as it thinks fit for performing the functions under this Act, and such sums shall be treated as expenditure payable out of the grants referred to in sub-section (1).

Grants by the State Government

(1) The State Government shall, after due appropriation made by Legislature by law in this behalf, pay to the State Commission by way of grants such sums of money as the State Government may think fit for being utilised for the purposes of this Act.

(2) The State Commission may spend such sums as it thinks fit for performing the functions under Chapter V, and such sums shall be treated as expenditure payable out of the grants referred to in sub-section (1).

Accounts and Audit

(1) The Commission shall maintain proper accounts and other relevant records and prepare an annual statement of accounts in such form as may be prescribed by the Central Government in consultation with the Comptroller and Auditor-General of India.

(2) The Accounts of the Commission shall be audited by the Comptroller and Auditor-General at such intervals as may be specified by him and any expenditure incurred in connection with such audit shall be payable by the Commission to the Comptroller and Auditor-General.

(3) The Comptroller and Auditor-General or any person appointed by him in connection with the audit of the accounts of the Commision

under this Act shall have the same rights and privileges and the authority in connection with such audit as the Comptroller and Auditor-General generally has in connection with the audit of Government ac counts and, in particular, shall have the right to demand the production of books, accounts, connected vouchers and other documents and papers and to inspect any of the offices of the Commission.

(4) The accounts of the Commission as certified by the Comptroller and Auditor-General or any other person appointed by him in this behalf, together with the audit report thereon shall be forwarded only to the Central Government by the Commission and the Central Government shall cause the audit report to be laid as soon as may be after it is received before each House of Parliament.

Accounts and Audit of State Commission

(1) The State Commission shall maintain proper accounts and other relevant records and prepare an annual statement of accounts in such form as may be prescribed by the State Government in consultation with the Comptroller and Auditor-General of India.

(2) The accounts of the State Commission shall be audited by the Comptroller and Auditor-General at such intervals as may be specified by him and any expenditure incurred in connection with such audit shall be payable by the State Commission to the Comptroller and Auditor-General.

(3) The Comptroller and Auditor-General or any person appointed by him in connection with the audit of the accounts of the State Commission under this Act shall have the same rights and privileges and the authority in connection with such audit as the Comptroller and Auditor-General generally has in connection with the audit of Government accounts and, in particular, shall have the right to demand the production of books, accounts, connected vouchers and other documents and papers and to inspect any of the offices of the State Commission.

(4) The accounts of the State Commission, as certified by the

Comptroller and Auditor-General or any other person appointed by him in this behalf, together with the audit report thereon, shall be forwarded annually to the State Government by the State Commission and the State Government shall cause the audit report to be laid, as soon as may be after it is received, before the State Legislature.

Chapter VIII

Miscellaneous

Matters not subject to jurisdiction of the Commission

(1) The Commission shall not inquire into any matter which is pending before a State Commission or any other Commission duly constituted under any law for the time being in force.

(2) The Commission or the State Commission shall not inquire into any matter after the expiry of one year from the date on which the act constituting violation of human rights is alleged to have been committed.

Constitution of special investigation teams

Notwithstanding anything contained in any other law for the time being in force, where the Government considers it necessary so to do, it may constitute one or more special investigation teams, consisting of such police officers as it thinks necessary for purposes of investigation and prosecution of offences arising out of violations of human rights.

Protection of action taken in good faith

No suit or other legal proceeding shall lie against the Central Government, State Government, Commission, the State Commission or any Member thereof or any person acting under the direction either of the Central Government, State Government, Commission or the State Commission in respect of anything which is in good faith done or intended to be done in pursuance of this Act or of any rules or any order made thereunder or in respect of the publication by or under the authority of the Central Government, State Government, Commission or the State Commission of any report paper or proceedings.

Members and officers to be public servants

Every Member of the Commission, State Commission and every officer appointed or authorised by the Commission or the State Commission to exercise functions under this Act shall be deemed to be a public servant within the meaning of section 21 of the Indian Penal Code.

Power of Central Government to make rules

(1) The Central Government may, by notification, make rules to carry out the provisions of this Act.

(2) In particular and without prejudice to the generality of the foregoing power, such rules may provide for all or any of the following matters namely :

    (a) the salaries and allowances and other terms and conditions of service of the Members under section 8;

    (b) the conditions subject to which other administrative, technical and scientific staff may be appointed by the Commission and the salaries and allowances of officers and other staff under sub-section (3) of section 11;

    (c) any other power of a civil court required to be prescribed under clause (f) of sub-section (1) of section 13;

    (d) the form in which the annual statement of accounts is to be prepared by the Commission under sub-section (1) of section 34; and

    (e) any other matter which has to be, or may be, prescribed.

(3) Every rule made under this Act shall be laid, as soon as may be after it is made, before each House of Parliament, while it is in session, for a total period of thirty days which may be comprised in one session or in two or more successive sessions, and if, before the expiry of the session immediately

following the session or the successive sessions aforesaid, both Houses agree in making any modification in the rule or both Houses agree that the rule should not be made, the rule shall thereafter have effect only in such modified form or be of no effect, as the case may be; so however, that any such modification or annulment shall be without prejudice to the validity of anything previously done under that rule.

Power of State Government to make rules

(1) The State Government may, by notification, make rules to carry out the provisions of this Act.

(2) In particular and without prejudice to the generality of the fore ing power, such rules may provide for all or any of the following matters, namely :

   (a) the salaries and allowances and other terms and conditions of service of the members under section 26;

   (b) the conditions subject to which other administrative, technical and scientific staff may be appointed by the State Commission and the salaries and allowances of officers and other staff under sub-section (3) of section 27;

   (c) the form in which the annual statement of accounts is to be prepared under sub-section (1) of section 35.

(3) Every rule made by the State Government under this section shall be laid, as soon as may be after it is made, before each House of the State Legislature where it consists of two Houses, or where such Legislature consists of one House, before that House.

Power to remove difficulties

(1) If any difficulty arises in giving effect to the provisions of this Act, the Central Government, may by order published in the Official Gazette, make such provisions, not inconsistent with the provisions of this Act as appear to it to be necessary or expedient for removing the difficulty.

   Provided that no such order shall be made after the expiry of the period of two years from the date of commencement of this Act.

(2) Every order made under this section shall, as soon as may be after it is made, be laid before each house of Parliament.

Repeal and Savings

(1) The Protection of Human Rights Ordinance, 1993 is hereby repealed.

(2) Notwithstanding such repeal, anything done or any action taken under the said Ordinance, shall be deemed to have been done or taken under the corresponding provisions of this Act.

Terrorist Atrocities on Women and Children in J&K, 1990-2004

Source : www.satp.org

Date	Place	Details of the incident
1990		
March 4	Baramula Town	Two girls are abducted, raped and later killed.
March 17	Takoora, Srinagar	The wife of a security force (SF) personnel is abducted, raped and later killed.
April 19	Hazratbal, Srinagar	An employee of the Medical Institute at Soura, Srinagar, is abducted, raped and later killed.
May 7	Karannagar, Srinagar	A woman is abducted and later killed at Karannagar chowk.
May 7	Sopore, Baramula district	A woman who was abducted along with her husband is raped and later killed. Her husband too was killed.
June 4	Trehgam, Kupwara district	A woman employee of the Government Girls High School, Trehgam, is abducted, raped and later killed.
June 4	Miskeenbagh, Srinagar	A girl is abducted, raped and killed.
June 17	Bano Mohalla, Srinagar	Two women are killed along with their husbands at their residence.
June 28	Darsu, Pulwama district	Two women are tortured and later killed at their residence in separate incidents.
July 18	Karannagar, Srinagar	A woman is killed at her residence.
August 13	Sopore, Baramula district	A teacher in the Education Department is raped at her residence and later killed.
October 14	Alikadal, Srinagar	Two women are killed along with their husbands at their residence.

1991		
January 15	Srinagar	A woman is killed and her daughter injured by a group of unidentified terrorists at their residence.
January 18	Hakbara, Baramula district	Unidentified terrorists abduct a girl after her refusal to marry a terrorist while her brother is killed.
March 21	Malik Sahab, Srinagar	A woman is abducted, raped and killed.
May 6	Bohripora, Kupwara district	A woman and her infant child are killed in indiscriminate fire by unidentified terrorists.
May 28	Pattan, Baramula district	A woman is raped and later killed.
June 29	Safakadal, Srinagar	A woman is killed and her body is thrown into Jhelum river.
July 19	Baramula	A woman attending a wedding is killed by unidentified terrorists while the ceremony is being performed.
July 31	Sonawar, Srinagar	A woman is killed when she raised an alarm on the abduction attempt of her husband.
August 6	Naibasti, Jammu	Unidentified terrorists kill a woman.
August 8	Karfoli Mohalla, Srinagar	A woman is abducted from her native village, gang raped and tortured to death in a deserted house.
August 25	Qamarwari, Srinagar	A woman is killed at the house of a relative who she was visiting along with her children.
August 27	Kemi, Chadoora, Budgam district	A woman is killed during a clash between a group of terrorists.
September 10	Batmaloo, Srinagar	Terrorists kill a woman at her residence.
September 23	Iqbal Park, Srinagar	A teenage girl, resident of Bandipur, Baramula, is abducted and gang raped for many days and her body was later found abandoned in a park at Srinagar.

October 1	Ahjan Road, Srinagar	The body of a young woman tortured and killed and bearing signs of rape is recovered from the lane.
October 17	Qamarwari, Srinagar	Unidentified terrorists kill a woman at a wedding ceremony.
October 17	Choontwari, Kupwara district	Terrorists intrude into the house of a civilian and attempt to abduct his wife. On resistance, she is shot at and injured.
December 17	Kokarhamam, Baramula district	A schoolgirl is kidnapped from the Government Girls Higher Secondary School, raped and killed. Her dead body is later recovered from Jhelum river.
December 19	Anantnag	Terrorists abduct a 17-year old girl from Ramban, Doda district. She is held captive for several days at Anantnag and physically assaulted. Security force personnel later rescue her.
1992		
January 5	Nowshera, Srinagar	The tortured dead body of a woman is recovered from a field.
January 23	Delina, Baramula district	Terrorists intruded into the residence of a civilian and kill his young son.
February 19	Yal Athmuqam, Anantnag	A boy is killed while resisting a terrorist attempt to abduct his father.
March 12	Sheen, Baramula	A woman is killed when she resists a terrorist attempt to abduct her.
March 17	Shopian, Pulwama district	A woman is tortured and later killed.
March 28	Tawheedganj, Baramula	Unidentified terrorists kill a woman at her residence.
March 30	Sultanpora, Budgam	Terrorists abduct the member of a rival group and kill his sister and brother, besides injuring his mother.
March 30	Naisarak, Srinagar	Unidentifed terrorists kill a civilian at his residence. His wife and daughter are raped and later killed.

April 8	Qamarwari, Srinagar	The dead body of a woman is recovered from Qamarwari area. She was earlier abducted.
April 12	Kunoo, Anantnag	Terrorists kill a woman at her residence.
April 15	Katamdanpor, Srinagar	Terrorists abduct a District Education Officer in Srinagar. However, she is released the next day.
May 2	Batmaloo, Srinagar	A woman and her young son are killed in a grenade attack by terrorists near a shop.
May 3	Magam, Baramulla	Terrorists abduct and later kill a woman.
May 4	Tekipora, Kupwara	Unidentified terrorists shoot dead a woman and her husband at their residence, alleging them to be 'informers'.
May 8	Anantnag	10 children are injured as terrorists hurl a grenade, which exploded on the road.
May 12	Chakia, Baramulla	Terrorists abduct a married woman and later killed three villagers and injured 15 more when they demonstrated against this action.
May 16	Srinagar	HuM terrrosits injure many women and ransack some houses when they came to a locality in search of JKLF cadres.
May 17	Eshalipora, Baramulla	Terrorists kill a woman, alleging her to be an 'informer'.
May 17	Ghanipora, Pulwama district	Terrorists abduct a young girl and hold her captive for two days till she is rescued by SFs. They later abducted the father and brother of the girl and killed them.
May 18	Safakadal, Srinagar	HuM terrorists abduct a woman and her daughter from their residence, alleging them to be instrumental in the arrest of their chief Mushtaq Ahmed Zargar alias Latrum. They also ransack the house and later set it ablaze.
May 20	Pirbagh, Srinagar	Following a clash between JKLF and HuM cadres, in which a terrorist is killed and two women injured, approximately 250 women demonstrate and raise anti-militant slogans. HuM cadres fire upon the women causing injuries to an unspecified number of them.

June 13	Baramulla	A girl is abducted, raped and later killed.
June 16	Qamarwari, Srinagar	A woman is killed along with her husband at her residence.
July 1	Nowpora, Anantnag	A seven-year old boy is killed when rival groups resorted to heavy firing in the village.
July 10	Baharabad, Baramulla	Two women and a child are injured when two rival groups clashed in the village.
July 19	Behrampora, Baramulla	A woman is killed and four others, including two children, injured when rival factions of terrorists resorted to an armed clash.
July 23	Kaloosa, Baramulla	Unidentified terrorists kill a woman at her residence.
August 9	Ganderbal, Srinagar	The body of a woman is recovered from Sindh river. She had earlier been abducted and tortured to death.
August 13	Tarzoo, Baramulla	A schoolboy is injured when rival terrorist groups resorted to firing in the village.
August 19	Trehgam, Kupwara district	A woman is killed at her residence along with her husband and father-in-law.
October 3	Khor, Baramulla	The body of a woman abducted earlier by terrorists is recovered from a field.
October 4	Duslipora, Budgam	A group of unidentified terrorists abduct a minor girl from the village. She is later rescued by SF personnel.
October 22	Zainakoot, Srinagar	Unidentified terrorists abduct a 12-year old girl along with her father.
November 24	Narayanbagh, Baramulla	A teenage girl is killed at her residence following resistance by inmates to the attempted abduction of her father by a group of unidentified terrorists.
December 2	New Colony, Srinagar	A woman is abducted from her residence along with her young son.
December 23	Srinagar	Two women are injured in grenade explosion at their residence.

1993		
January 1	Barzulla, Srinagar	Two women are hanged to death along with a lone male member present in the house.
January 25	Marhama, Kupwara district	Terrorists kill a mother and her daughter as well as a male member of the family.
January 29	Kupwara district	Three women are killed along with two male members of the family.
February 5	Kupwara	A woman and her young son are killed by terrorists in their house.
February 9	Gadigarh, Jammu	A young woman is killed at her father's clinic. The doctor is also shot at and injured.
February 13	Baramulla	A woman is abducted, raped and later killed. Her dead body is recovered from Jhelum river.
February 14	Srinagar	The body of a girl abducted earlier from Nadihal (Baramulla) is recovered from the roadside.
February 15	Baramulla	Unidentified terrorists abduct a civilian and kill his young son.
March 6	Anantnag	Terrorists fire at the residence of a civilian, killing a woman and injuring eight others, including two children.
April 1	Baramulla	Terrorists intrude into the residence house of a civilian and kill his wife.
April 3	Srinagar	A woman is killed as terrorists fire upon shops to enforce a hartal in the State capital.
April 6	Anantnag	Unidentified terrorists kill a woman at her residence.
May 7	Kishtwar, Doda	A three-year old child is charred to death when a house is set ablaze by unidentified terrorists during night.
May 11	Ganderbal, Srinagar	A woman is killed by a group of unidentified terrorists.
May 11	Shahan Mohalla, Baramulla	The dead body of a woman, who was killed by terrorists, is recovered in Shahan Mohalla.

May 12	Doda town	A woman and her daughter are abducted and set free three days later, after being sexually assaulted and tortured.
May 21	Baramulla	Terrorists kill a woman at her residence.
May 21	Anantnag	Unidentifed terrorists kill a woman at her residence.
May 29	Srinagar	Terrorists abduct a woman, her husband and daughter. The women are released after 10 days in captivity during which they are sexually assaulted.
May 29	Baramulla	A woman is abducted, tortured and later killed by terrorists.
June 4	Doda town	A woman is abducted, raped and later killed.
June 8	Baramulla	A woman and her husband are killed in Shahgund.
June 9	Pulwama	A woman is dragged out of her residence and later killed at Ratnipora.
June 10	Srinagar	A woman is abducted from her residence, sexually abused and later killed at Kangan.
Jue 13	Lal Bazar, Srinagar	SFs recover the dead body of a woman abducted by terrorists earlier, on May 23, 1993, and abused sexually.
June 17	Watalkadal, Srinagar	A female employee of Doordarshan is abducted in Srinagar, sexually abused and later killed. Her dead body is recovered from Watalkadal.
July 6	Trehgam, Kupwara	The dead body of a woman is recovered from Trehgam.
July 23	Srinagar	Unidentified terrorists kill a girl and throw her body on the road.
August 1	Anantnag town	Two girls are hanged to death at their residence by terrorists.
August 1	Hajam, Baramulla	Terrorists kill a young girl at her residence.
August 13	Rathpora, Kupwara district	Terrorists barge into the residnce of a civilian and kill him and his wife.

August 21	Kishtwar, Doda	The wife of BJP leader Manmohan Gupta is seriously injured when she is shot at by unidentified terrorists at her residence.
August 22	Ushroo, Pulwama district	A young boy is killed and his body is recovered from a riverbed.
August 25	Bandipur, Baramulla	Terrorists kill a woman and her husband at their residence.
September 1	Kaloosa, Baramulla	Unidentified terrorists kill a woman at her residence.
September 10	Anantnag town	Two women are killed along with four other family members in an explosion set-off by terrorists at their residence.
September 13	Ichgam, Budgam	A lady constable and a woman are abducted. The woman is sexually abused for three days and then manages to escape. The lady constable is subsquently rescued by SFs.
September 14	Alasteng, Srinagar	A woman is killed and her daughter injured by unidentified terrorists.
September 15	Srinagar	A woman is seriously injured in a mine-explosion trigerred by terrorists near an Army vehicle.
September 17	Aloochibagh, Srinagar	A woman is killed during an armed clash between two rival groups of terrorists.
September 21	Nowhatta, Srinagar	10 civilians, including two women, are injured in a grenade attack on an SF post.
September 24	Gugloosa, Kupwara district	A young boy is killed in a grenade explosion.
October 6	Tral, Pulwama	A seven-year old boy is killed and his parents injured by unidentified terrorists.
October 8	Kishtwar, Doda	A woman and her husband are killed at their residence.
October 13	Pulwama district	SF personnel in a search operation rescue an abducted girl.
October 15	Atholi, Doda	Four young girls are abducted and are later rescued by SFs.

October 20	Tral, Pulwama	A young boy is killed when a grenade explodes in his hand. Terrorists had forced him to hurl the grenade at an SFs convoy.
October 20	Doda Town	Three school children are injured in a grenade attack on an SFs picket.
October 21	Dialgam, Anantnag	A young boy is seriously injured when unidentified terrorists intrude into his residence and fire at him.
October 30	Kupwara town	A young girl and her father are killed at her residence.
November 3	Chandanwari, Baramulla	Terrorists kill a girl at her house.
November 9	Budgam	A young girl, abducted and brought to the Valley from an undisclosed location and sexually abused, is rescued from a terrorist hideout by SFs.
November 11	Baramulla	A woman is killed when terrorists hurl a grenade on the road.
November 11	Poonch	A woman is killed in an explosion caused by terrorists on the road.
November 14	Shalakadal, Srinagar	The highly decomposed body of a woman is recovered from the deserted house of a Hindu migrant. She had been abducted on July 6, 1991, while on her way home from office.
November 21	Sopore, Baramulla	A woman is killed and her dead body was thrown on the bank of Wular lake in Bandipore.
November 22	Baramulla	Unidentifed terrorists kill a woman and injure three of her children at her residence.
November 26	Baramulla	A woman is killed in the crossfire between two rival terrorist groups.
November 26	Budgam	Two women and four others of their family are killed.
November 26	Kupwara	Unidentified terrorists intrude into a house and commence indiscriminate firing killing two women, an infant and three others of the family.

December 22	Anantnag	A child is killed and two more children injured when terrorists set off an explosion in a village hut.
1994		
January 13	Zerobridge, Srinagar	A young girl is killed in the crossfire in a group-clash.
January 23	Qazigund, Anantnag	A woman is tortured to death by a group of unidentified terrorists.
February 4	Baramulla	SF personnel rescue a girl abducted earlier by terrorists.
February 7	Bichroo, Anantnag	Two women are killed and their bodies thrown on the road.
February 8	Shalakadal, Srinagar	The highly decmposed body of a woman, tortured to death earlier, is recovered from the vacant house of a Hindu migrant.
February 9	Bongund, Anantnag	SF personnel discover the dead body of a woman tortured earlier along with her father.
February 9	Baramulla town	Terrorists intrude into the house of a civilian and seriously injure a woman.
February 14	Trehgam, Kupwara	A woman is fired at by unidentified terrrosits and injured seriously.
February 27	Bonyar, Baramulla	The dead body of an unidentified women killed by terrorists is recovered from river Jhelum.
March 1	Ganderbal, Srinagar	A retired police personnel is killed and his wife injured by terrorists at their residence.
March 5	Baramulla	A woman and three other members of her family are killed in a targeted grenade explosion inside their residence.
March 7	Rambagh, Srinagar	The dead body of a young girl abducted earlier is recovered from a vacant house.
March 15	Tankanwari, Srinagar	The dead body of a woman abducted earlier by terrorists on February 2, 1994 is recovered from the river isde.
April 1	Bagyass, Chattabal area, Srinagar	During a clash between cadres of rival terrorist groups at Bagyass Chattabal, a woman is killed.

April 3	Baramulla	A woman is abducted, tortured and later killed.
April 5	Batmaloo, Srinagar	Terrorists intrude into the residence of a civilian and kill his daughter and abduct another.
April 11	Kamah sector, Kupwara district	A woman is seriously injured in an explosion set-off ar her house by unidentified terrorists.
April 19	Pulwama Town	A 10-year old boy is killed in a grenade attack at the local bus stand.
April 23	Baramulla	A five-year old girl is killed in the crossfire between rival terrorist groups.
April 25	Srinagar	A five-year old girl is injured the crossfirig during an armed clash between rival terrorist groups.
April 27	Langanbal, Anantnag	The strangulated body of a woman is recovered from Langanbal village, Anantnag-Pahalgam road. She is earlier abducted and tortured to death.
April 29	Budgam	A woman and her husband are killed by unidentified terrorists at their residence.
April 29	Dardpora, Baramulla	A young girl is killed and four others are injured in crossfiring during a clash between rival terrorist groups.
May 3	Anantnag	A woman is abducted and later killed.
May 5	Budgam	A young girl is abducted from her residence in Anwarshah locality.
May 8	Sopore, Baramulla	The dead body of girl abducted earlier is recovered.
May 8	Baramulla	A woman is fired at by terrorists and injured seriously.
May 12	Nowhatta, Srinagar	Terrorists attempt to abduct the daughter of former Minister Ali Mohd Sagar from her relative's residence. Upon resistance from the inmates, the terrorists shoot at her and inflict serious injuries.
May 30	Bhaderwa-h, Doda	A woman is killed in the crossfire between unidentified terrorists and PSO's of a Bharatiya Janata Party (BJP) leader in Sungti.

June 17	Baramulla	A woman is injured seriously by a group of unidentified terrorists.
June 20	Doda	A woman is sexually abused by unidentified terrorists, who barged into her house. They also injure her father and ransack the house.
June 20	Kishtwar, Doda	Two girls are abducted from by unidentified terrorists.
June 24	Batpora, Baramulla	Unidentified terrorists kill a woman at her residence.
June 26	Tangmarg, Baramulla	Terrorists storm the historical Baba Reshi Shrine and resort to indiscriminate firing on pilgrims injuring two women.
June 26	Gandoh,- Doda	The dead body of an 18-year old girl abducted earlier and raped by unidentified terrorists is recovered.
July 3	Madwan, Baramulla	A woman abducted earlier by terrorists is rescued by SFs.
July 5	Trehgam, Kupwara district	A woman is abducted and later tortured to death. Her dead body is recovered from the bus stand.
July 6	Reshi Muqam, Baramulla	Terrorists injure into the house of a widow and kill her, besides injuring her son.
July 15	Lalpora, Kupwara	A woman is killed and another injured in a roadside attack on them by terrorists.
July 16	Habak, Srinagar	A woman is abducted and tortured to death by terrorists.
July 18	Baramulla	A civilian is killed and his young daughter injured at their residence.
July 24	Pakherpo- ra, Baramulla	A woman and her daughter are abducted from a hospital compound. Later, they are tortured to death and their bodies thrown in the fields.
August 2	Kothibagh, Srinagar	A student of Government Women's college is killed and two others injured when terrorists hurl a grenade on an SF vehicle near the college gate.

August 5	Nowshera, Rajouri	The dead body of a woman tortured to death by unidentified terrorists is recovered from the village.
August 10	Kanimazar, Srinagar	Two children are killed and three others injured in a grenade explosion.
August 22	Shopian, Pulwama	A woman is killed and 10 others injured, following a grenade attack by terrorists on an SFs party.
August 22	Dangerpora, Baramulla	Terrorists intrude into the residence of a civilian and kill a woman.
August 25	Noorbagh, Srinagar	Two women are injured following a grenade attack by unidentified terrorists on an SFs party.
August 27	Bagh-e-Mehtab, Srinagar	Militants intrude into the house of Ab. Ghani Bhat and shoot his wife dead, besides injuring two others.
September 20	Pulwama	Terrorists kill a woman, injure her husband and abduct their nine-year old child.
September 22	Doda	An 11-year old Hindu girl is killed inside her residence along with her brothers and grandfather.
September 25	Sopore, Baramulla	Unidentified terrorists kill a civilian and his wife at their residence.
September 26	Budgam	Terrorists kill a woman at her house.
September 26	Doda	Unidentified terrorists kill a young student.
October 18	Kachihama, Kupwara	Two women are killed in a grenade attack on their residence.
November 1	Hakbara, Baramulla	Unidentified terrorists kill a civilian, torture his wife and abduct his son.
November 16	Baramulla	Terrorists kill a young boy outside his house.
November 18	Doda	A woman and an 11-year old girl and another are killed at their farm.

November 22	Khanyar, Srinagar	Terrorists kill a Muslim woman shopkeeper for refusing to pay money and for resisting abduction.
December 1	Chanpora, Srinagar	A woman is killed in a grenade attack on her residence.
December 7	Kandipora, Kupwara	A woman and a boy are injured in an explosion set off outside their house by terrorists.
December 10	Doda	A woman is seriously injured and her husband shot dead by unidentified terrorists, who intrud into their house and open indiscriminate fire.
December 20	Sogam, Kupwara	Terrorists kill a woman at her residence.
1995		
January 1	Telbal, Srinagar	A woman is killed in an explosion set off by terrorists at a local bus stop.
January 20	Maulana Azad Stadium, Jammu	Over 30 school children are seriously injured when unidentified terrorists set off three explosions at the Republic Day celebrations in the stadium.
January 25	Kupwara	Terrorists abduct a woman and sexually abuse her. She is later rescued by SFs during a search operation.
February 8	Kulgam, Anantnag	Terrorists kill a woman at her residence.
February 14	Baramulla	A nurse at a local hospital is killed and her mother injured.
February 17	Ganderbal, Srinagar	A young boy is killed outside his house in Wakoora village.
February 20	Rajbagh, Srinagar	A woman is abducted, sexually abused and later burnt to death.
February 24	Baramulla	A woman and four others are killed in the crossfirie during an armed clash between rival terrorist groups.
February 26	Kamalkote, Baramulla	A civilian is killed and a woman injured by unidentified terrorists.

March 4	Chowkibal, Kupwara	A woman, her daughter and her husband are killed in a grenade attack on their residence.
March 4	Qazigund, Anantnag	A civilian and his wife are killed at their residence.
March 10	Zakoora, Srinagar	Terrorists kill a woman at her house.
March 12	Padgampora, Pulwama	Two teenage girls are injured in heavy firing on their houses by terrorists.
March 13	Kulgam, Anantnag	Unidentified terrorists kill a woman.
March 28	Braripora, Srinagar	Unidentified terrorists injure a woman in an attack on her residence.
May 4	Anantnag	A woman is tortured and later killed by a group of unidentified terrorists.
May 5	Budgam	Two women are killed in an explosion in their village.
May 11	Wanganpora, Srinagar	A young boy is killed outside his house.
May 17	Baramulla	Terrorists kill a civilian and his daughter at their residence.
May 19	Pulwama	Terrorists kill a woman at her residence.
June 1	Lal Bazar, Srinagar	Unidentifed terrorists abduct a woman and her brother.
June 2	PanthaChowk, Srinagar	The dead body of a girl tortured to death by terrorists is recovered.
June 7	Srinagar	A four-year old girl is abducted by unidentified terrorists from her house and later killed.
June 9	Doda	A woman is abducted by unidentified terrorists from her house, gang-raped and tortured to death. Her body is later recovered in the forests.
June 22	Pralpora, Pulwama	A 10-year old boy is killed inside his house and his father injured.

June 29	Srinagar	A woman is abducted and later killed.
June 29	Sheikhpora, Kupwara	A woman is killed inside her residence.
July 3	Kanigund, Anantnag	Terrorists intrude into the house of a civilian and kill his wife.
July 10	Budgam	A teenage girl is killed at her house.
July 15	Kupwara	A civilian and his wife are killed by a group of unidentified terrorists.
July 20	Kathidarwaza, Srinagar	Two girls are abducted by terrorists from their locality.
August 12	Bijbehara, Anantnag	A young boy is killed and his mother injured in an explosion in their house.
August 13	Kupwara	A woman is killed at her residence.
August 23	Awantipur, Pulwama	A schoolboy is abducted by unidentified terrrosits and later killed.
October 24	Baramulla	Two women are injured in an explosion set off by terrorists in their village.
October 29	Badipur, Budgam	Terrorists abduct a woman and her son and later kill the woman.
October 29	Noorpora, Pulwama	A student is killed outside a mosque by a group of unidentified terrorists.
September 3	Pulwama	Terrorists kill a woman when she resists an abduction attempt.
September 5	Wakoora, Srinagar	Unidentified terrorists kill a young girl and three other family members.
September 11	Ganderbal, Srinagar	The dead body of a woman killed by terrrosits earlier is recovered from the riverside.
September 11	Mirgund, Baramulla	A civilian and his daughter are killed at their house.
September 19	Kakpora, Pulwama	A schoolboy is killed by terrorists in the village.

September 23	Shangas, Anantnag	A woman is killed at hre residence by unidentified terrorists.
September 23	Tankipora, Srinagar	The dead body of a woman killed earlier by terrrosits is recovered near the Deputy Commissioner's office.
October 5	Srinagar	A woman is abducted and later killed while her son is injured.
October 6	Hazratbal, Srinagar	A woman lecturer in Kashmir University is shot at by terrorists and injured.
October 7	Kupwara	Unidentified terrorists kill a woman at her house.
October 9	Nowpora, Srinagar	Terrorists kill a woman in the village.
October 12	Kralkhud, Srinagar	The dead body of an elderly woman killed earlier by terrorists is recovered from the village.
October 12	Ahmednagar, Srinagar	The dead body of an elderly woman killed earlier by terrorists is recovered from the village.
October 12	Khanyar, Srinagar	Unidentified terrorists abduct a woman from her house.
October 15	Bana Mohalla, Srinagar	Terrorists set ablaze the house of a civilian and kill one of his daughters.
October 17	Sheikh Mohalla, Srinagar	Two women are injured in indiscriminate firing by terrorists.
October 19	Rajbagh, Sriangar	A young boy is killed and two others are injured by terrorists.
October 19	Nowhatta, Srinagar	A Muslim woman is shot dead by militants at her house.
October 24	Anantnag	Two women are injured in an explosion at their residence.
October 24	Mirhama, Anantnag	Two women are injured when terrorists open indiscriminate fire.
October 25	Kupwara	The dead body of a woman killed earlier by terrorists is recovered from the forests.

October 26	Nagin, Srinagar	A lady medical practitioner is abducted by unidentified terrorists from her house and released the next day.
October 27	Sheikhpora, Baramulla	A woman is killed and three others are when unidentified terrorists open indiscriminate fire.
October 31	Poonch	Unidentified terrorists intrude into the residence of a civilian and injure his daughter.
November 1	Nowabad, Baramulla	A young girl is abducted and later killed by terrorists.
November 1	Qazibad, Anantnag	Terrorists abduct the daughter of senior politician Ghulam Nabi Sofi and two other inmates from his house and set ablaze the house.
November 2	Sopore, Baramulla	Unidentifed terrorists rape a woman at her residence.
November 14	Anantnag	A woman is killed by terrorists following her resistance to the abduction of her husband.
November 15	Bagh-e-Islamia, Baramulla	A woman is abducted from her residence.
November 16	Budgam	HuM terrorists abduct a woman from her residence.
November 23	Kupwara	A woman is killed in the forests while collecting firewood.
December 1	Anantnag	A woman is killed at her house by terrorists.
December 2	Pampore, Pulwama	The dead body of a woman killed earlier by terrorists is recovered from a farm.
December 3	Anantnag town	Two women and an infant, besides nine others, are killed in an explosion set off by terrorists at the Old Bus Stand.
December 25	Naqashpora, Srinagar	Terrorists kill a woman at hre residence.
1996		
January 3	Anantnag	Two girls are injured in armed clashes between terrorists of two rival groups in Katrosoo and Kanchwan villages.

January 12	Poshpora, Pulwama	A teenage girl is fired at by terrorists and seriously injured, while her two brothers are killed.
January 19	Awantipur, Pulwama	A woman is killed at her house.
January 21	Kupwara	A woman is killed at her residence.
February 4	Bagh-e- Mehtab, Srinagar	A woman is killed after she was abducted along with 11 other persons of whom three abductees were also tortured and decapitated.
February 5	Ganderbal, Srinagar	A woman is injured while her husband is killed in a grenade attack by terrorists on her residence.
February 10	Pulwama	A teenagedgirl is killed at her residence.
February 10	Pulwama	A teenage girl is killed at her residence.
February 15	Bohrikadal, Srinagar	A woman is killed at her residence.
February 21	Dangarpora, Pulwama	A 10-year old girl is killed when terrorists hurl an explosive device at the residence of a civilian.
March 7	Natipora, Srinagar	Militants kill a woman travelling with her husband in a car.
March 24	Lachipora, Kupwara	A woman and her husband are killed at their house.
March 26	Srinagar	A teenage girl and her father are killed in a houseboat.
April 6	Ratnipora, Pulwama	A woman and her two children are killed in a grenade attack on their house.
April 7	Baramulia	A woman is killed at her residence.
April 10	Anantnag	Unidentified terrorists kill a woman and injure another.
April 11	Kupwara	A civilian and his daughter are killed at their residence.
April 13	Anantnag	A woman is shot at and injured seriously.

May 1	Kupwara	Terrorists kill a woman and her son-in-law at her residence.
May 3	Khanyar, Srinagar	A young student is killed outside his house.
May 3	Rajouri	Unidentified terrorists intrude into the residence of local Congress-I leader Ayub Pehalwan and kill his wife and injure three others in indiscriminate firing.
May 5	Baramulla	Unidentified terrorists kill a tennage girl and five others at her house.
May 5	Baramulla	A young boy is killed at his residence.
May 6	Budgam	Terrorists abduct a young girl from her house.
May 7	Kupwara	A nine-year boy is killed in an explosion.
June 1	Anantnag	A woman is killed and three others are injured in an attack by terrorists on a hospital vehicle they were travelling in.
June 14	Srinagar	A woman and her brother are killed while her infant is injured at their residence.
June 17	Srinagar	A young girl and her father are killed at her house.
June 19	Daulatabad, Srinagar	Terrorists intrude into the house of a woman and shoot her dead.
June 21	Srinagar	A young girl is abducted from her house.
June 24	Srinagar	A woman is killed in the crossfire bwetween rival terrorist groups in the locality.
June 25	Pulwama	A young boy is shot dead at his house.
June 30	Anantnag	A woman is killed when terrorists intrude into the village and resort to indiscriminate firing.
July 7	Anantnag	The decomposed body of a woman killed earlier by terrorists is recovered from the village.
July 7	Pinglina, Pulwama	Terrorists intrude into the house of a civilian and shoot at his daughter when she resists an abduction attempt.
July 15	Regal Chowk, Srinagar	Five women are among 13 persons injured when terrorists hurl a grenade on a SF vehicle, which exploded on the road.

July 16	Safakadal, Srinagar	A leading National Conference activist is killed and a nine-year old boy is injured.
July 28	Rajouri	The wife and daughter of a BJP leader are injured when unidentified terrorists hurl a grenade at his residence.
August 14	Anantnag	Unidentified terrorists kill a woman.
August 17	Pulwama	Terrorists kill Congress-I leader Syed Shah's daughter at their house.
August 17	Anantnag	Terrorists abduct a young girl.
August 20	Anantnag	Three girl students are injured in indiscriminate firing by unidentified terrorists.
September 6	Hajan, Baramulla	Terrorists intrude into the house of a civilian and resort to indiscriminate firing killing his wife and two sons.
September 7	Tujjar, Baramulla	Two young boys are killed and five others injured in indiscriminate firing by terrorists on a school compound.
September 7	Kupwara	Terrorists kill a 10-year old boy and inflict gun shot injuries on two other children.
September 11	Nowgam, Anantnag	A woman is killed in a grenade attack by terrorists at a public meeting.
September 18	Chathpora, Baramulla	A woman is killed and injured by unidentified terrorists.
September 21	Doda	A young boy is abducted by unidentified terrorists from his residence and later tortured to death. His body with torture marks is recovered from the forests, five kms away from the town.
September 23	Pulwama	The dead body of a girl student abducted earlier by terrorists is recovered from the roadside.
September 23	Baramulla	The dead body of a girl killed earlier by terrorists is recovered from Jhelum river in Baramulla town, near the Police Lines.

September 26	Srinagar	A civilian and his wife are killed at their residence.
September 26	Anantnag	A woman and her father are killed for resisting an abduction attempt.
October 7	Khargund, Kupwara	A woman is killed at her residence.
October 8	Pulwama	A woman is killed and her daughter injured by unidentified terrorists.
October 11	Dardipora, Kupwara	Unidentified terrorists intrude into the house of a civilian and kill his two daughters.
October 11	Kupwara	A woman is killed and her daughter injured at their house.
October 12	Jawaharnagar, Srinagar	A woman is shot at and injured at her house.
October 17	Nawbagh, Anantnag	A woman is killed and her father injured at their residence.
October 23	Soti, Doda	Unidentified terrorists assault the sister of former Union Minister Ghulam Nabi Azad.
October 27	Fatehpur, Anantnag	A woman is shot dead at her house.
October 28	Idgah, Srinagar	A Deupty Superintendent of Police is killed and his wife injured in a terrroist ambush on their vehicle.
October 28	Lakhipora, Anantnag	A woman is killed at her house by unidentified terrorists.
November 6	Khumryal, Kupwara	A woman is shot at and injured at her residence.
November 12	Srinagar	The dead body of a young girl killed earlier by terrorists is recovered from Jhelum river.
November 14	Baramulla	A girl is fired upon by terrorists in her house and injured seriously.
November 18	Ludna, Doda	Two children are killed in an IED explosion at their farm.

November 20	Gopalpora, Anantang	The dead body of a girl killed earlier by terrorists is recovered from the road-side near her house.
December 5	Baramulla	Terrorists intrude into a house and shoot at two women, injuring them both.
December 8	Rainawari, Srinagar	Terrorists abduct a girl from her house.
December 12	Nassaupora, Pulwama	A woman is shot at and injured at her residence.
December 12	Aishmuqam, Anantnag	A woman and her husband are killed at their house.
December 14	Beerwah, Budgam	Terrorists abduct a girl from her house.
December 17	Baramulla	A girl is shot at and injured by unidentified terrorists.
December 18	Kupwara	Terrorists intrude into the house of a civilian and shoot at his daughter injuring her seriously.
December 23	Rakhpora, Pulwama	A young boy is abducted and tortured to death by unidentified terrorists.
1997		
January 13	Sopore, Baramulla	Terrorists kill a woman at her house.
January 29	Karfali Mohalla, Srinagar	A girl is abducted by unidentified terrorists and raped before being strangulated to death.
February 1	Baramulla	Terrorists intrude into the house of a civilian and kill his son, besides injuring his wife.
February 11	Pulwama	Two women are killed and seven others injured in an explosion set off by terrorists in a house.
February 11	Kalamdanpora, Srinagar	SF personnel rescue two minor girls abducted earlier by terrorists from their house.

March 2	Budgam	A woman is shot dead at her house by terrorists.
March 8	Kishtwar, Doda	A woman is killed and her husband injured at their residence.
March 20	Kupwara	A woman is shot dead at her house by terrorists.
March 23	Budgam	A girl is killed and her father injured by terrorists.
April 5	Dal Lake, Srinagar	The dead bead body of a boy killed earlier by terrorists is recovered.
April 9	Baramulla	The dead body of a woman killed earlier by terrorists is recovered.
April 13	Poonch	Unidentified terrorists kill a woman at her residence.
April 15	Rajouri	A woman is gang raped by a group of unidentified terrorists.
April 25	Srinagar	A group of 10 unidentified terrorists kill four persons, including two women.
May 4	Anantnag	Two girls and an SF personnel are killed by terrorists during a search operation.
May 6	Dal Lake, Srinagar	A released terrorist abducts a woman.
May 19	Chandanwari, Baramulla	Terrorists abduct a woman.
May 20	Sopore, Baramulia	Terrorists abduct a woman.
May 29	Kupwara	A teenaged girl is killed at her residence
June 2	Beerwah, Budgam	A woman is killed at her residence
June 9	Beoli, Doda	A woman is killed by a group of unidentified terrorists when she resists an attempt to abduct her husband.
June 10	Nowhata, Srinagar	A schoolgirl is abducted by terrorists.
June 12	Anantnag	A woman and another person are killed by a group of terrorists.

June 16	Budgam	A woman is abducted by unidentified terrorists.
June 23	Anantnag	HuM terrrosits kill a woman and injure her son.
June 30	Aloochi Bagh, Srinagar	Terrorists abduct a woman.
July 7	Budgam	A 12-year old girl is abducted.
July 8	Yaripora, Kupwara	A woman is shot at and injured. Terrorists also loot her personal belongings.
July 8	Surankote, Poonch	Unidentified terrorists kill a woman and set her house ablaze, suspecting her to be an SF informer.
July 13	Baramulla	Two women abducted earlier by terrorists are killed.
July 16	Kokernag, Anantnag	A woman is shot dead by militants.
July 17	Anantnag	A schoolboy is shot dead by a group of unidentified terrorists.
July 20	Rajouri	A woman is killed by unidentified terrorists.
July 25	Baramulla	A woman is shot dead in her house.
August 8	Batpora, Anantnag	The dead body of a woman with torture marks is recovered.
August 20	Kupwara	Terrorists kill a woman and her husband.
September 22	Anantnag	Terrrorists intrude into the house of an IuM activist and kill his daughter.
October 29	Anantnag	Terrorists abduct and later kill a woman relative of an Ikhwani.
November 5	Kupwara	A woman and her daughter are killed at their residence.
November 14	Ichgam, Budgam	The dead body of a woman abducted earlier by terrorists is recovered.
November 20	Qazigund, Anantnag	A woman is killed in indiscriminate firing by terrorists at her residence.
December 1	Doda	Unidentified terrorists intrude into the house of a civilian and kill his wife and daughter.

December 13	Banihal, Doda	A group of unidentified terrorists kill a woman at her residence.
December 20	Handwara, Kupwara	Two women sustain injuries in indiscriminate firing in the village by terrorists.
December 22	Taranwali Jungle, Poonch	A group of five terrorists intrude into the house of a civilian and kill his 16-year old son.
December 26	Kupwara	Unidentified terrorists abduct a 19-year girl.
* Data source : www.satp.org		

Figure-1 Yearwise Summary of NHRC and Non-NHRC Cases Received by the Army

Ser No.	YEAR	NHRC		TOTAL	NON-NHRC		TOTAL	Overall Total
		J & K	NE		J & K	NE		
1	1994	11	06	17	03	--	03	20
2	1995	12	12	24	03	03	06	30
3	1996	28	15	43	02	04	06	49
4	1997	119	20	139	24	35	59	198
5	1998	26	21	47	27	31	58	105
6	1999	48	21	69	77	22	99	168
7	2000	141	10	151	35	19	54	205
8	2001	79	21	100	38	08	46	146
9	2002	142	24	166	08	02	10	176
10	2003	12	20	32	04	04	08	40
11	2004	08	27	35	05	04	09	44
12	2005	21	14	35	13	01	14	49
13	2006	11	18	29	10	01	11	40
14	2007	17	15	32	10	06	16	48
15	2008	15	13	28	02	01	03	31
16	2009	13	32	45	08	01	09	54
17	2010	08	22	30	10	07	17	47
	TOTAL	711	311	1022	279	149	428	1450

Decreasing Trend

* Data Source : Army HQs

Figure-2 Summary of Punishment for Human Rights Violations from 1994 to 31 Dec 2010

Ser No	Type	Pers Punished Offrs Jcos Or			Total
1	Cashiered/Dismissal With Ri 8-14 Years	--	--	10	10
2	Cashiered / Dismissal With Ri 1-8 Years	02	--	02	04
3	Dismissal With Ri Upto 1 Year	--	--	06	06
4	Dismissal From Service	01	--	02	03
5	Ri In Military Custody	--	--	09	09
6	Other Punishments	19	04	04	27
7	Total Pers Punished	22	04	33	59

FIGURE 3 Summary Of Punishment For Human Rights Violations From 1994 To 31 Dec 2010

Ser No	Type	Pers Punished Offrs Jcos Or			Total
1	Termination Of Service	01	--	02	03
2	Dismissal With Life Imprisonment	--	--	01	01
3	Cashiered / Dismissal With Ri 8-14 Years	--	--	14	14
4	Cashiered / Dismissal With Ri 1-8 Yearsfrom Service	01	--	07	08
5	Dismissal From Service	--	--	02	02
6	Ri In Military Custody	--	01	10	11
7	Other Punishments	14	07	10	31
	Total Pers Punished	16	08	46	70

Comd	Army	Rr	Ar	Total
NC (J&K)	21	38	--	59
	41	09	20	70

Figure 4- Summary of Allegation of Human Rights Violations and Percentage of True and False Cases from 1994 To 31 Dec 2010 - J&K and Northeast

1	Total Cases Received	1450
2	Total Cases Investigated	1404
3	Number Of Allegations False / Baseless	1350(96%)
4	Number Of Allegations Found True	54 (4%)

* Tables 1 to 4

Bibliography

BOOKS

War Against Insurgency and Terrorism in Kashmir by Lt Gen (Retd) YM Bammi, Natraj Publishers, Dehradun.

Kashmir – The Storm Center of the World by Bal Raj Madhok, A Ghosh, Publisher, Published in the United States of America.

My Frozen Turbulence in Kashmir by Jagmohan, Allied Publishers, New Delhi.

Low Intensity Conflict in India by Lt Gen (Retd) VK Nayar, USI, New Delhi.

Low Intensity Conflicts in India by Lt Gen Vivek Chadha, Sage Publications, New Delhi.

Military Operations in Kashmir : Insurgency at Charar-e-Sharief by GN Gauhar, Manas, New Delhi.

Death of a Dream : A Terrorist's Tale by Aditya SInha, Harper Collins, New Delhi.

Protection of Human Rights by Khwaja Abdul Muntaqim, Law Publishers (India) Pvt Ltd, Allahabad.

Study and Practice of Military Law by GK Sharma and MS Jaswal, Deep and Deep Publications, New Delhi.

Human Rights and the Indian Army by Air Cmde RV Kumar, AVSM and Gp Capt BP Sharma, Sterling Publishers PVt Ltd, New Delhi.

An Introduction to Politics by Sibnath Chakravarty, Modern Book Agency Pvt Ltd, Calcutta.

Human Rights Training Vol 2 by S Subramanian, Manas Publications, New Delhi.

The Impact of Human Rights Law on Armed Forces, by Peter Rowe, Cambridge University Press, Cambridge.

JOURNALS

Maj Harcharan Singh, "Human Rights and the Armed Forces in Low Intensity Conflict Operations", Journal of the United Service Institution of India, Vol CXXV, No.521, July-September 1995, pp 323-334.

Capt DJS Chahal, "Human Rights and the Armed Forces in Low Intensity Conflict Operations", Journal of the United Service Institution of India, Vol CXXV, No.522, October-December 1995, pp 459-472.

Cdr AN Sonsale, "Counter Insurgency and Human Rights", Journal of the United Service Institution of India, Vol CXXXIX, No.536, April-June 1999, pp 212-223.

Maj Praveen Badrinath, "Psychological Impact of Protracted Service in Low Intensity Conflict Operations (LICO) on Armed Forces Personnel : Causes and Remedies". Journal of the United Service Institution of India, Vol CXXXIII, No.551, January-March 2003.

Maj Gen Nilendra Kumar, "Judiciary : Troops in Counter Terrorism Tasks", Journal of the United Service Institution of India, Vol CXXXIV, No.555, January-March 2004, pp 101-110.

Dr Sudhir S Bloerie, "Kashmir: Summers of Disruption", Journal of the United Service Institution of India, Vol CXLI, No.583, January-March 2011, pp 22-28.

PAPERS

Narender Kumar, "Jammu and Kashmir : The Emerging Contours and the Way Ahead, Centre for Land Warfare Studies, Manekshaw Paper No.21, 2010.

www.ingramcontent.com/pod-product-compliance
Lightning Source LLC
Chambersburg PA
CBHW070809300326
41914CB00078B/1918/J